THE FRUIT OF A SPIRIT-LED LEADER

Characteristics of Jesus Displayed in Business through the Power of the Holy Spirit

KNEISHA SANDERS

WestBow Press
A DIVISION OF THOMAS NELSON
& ZONDERVAN

Copyright © 2020 Kneisha Sanders.

All rights reserved. No part of this book may be used or reproduced by any means, graphic, electronic, or mechanical, including photocopying, recording, taping or by any information storage retrieval system without the written permission of the author except in the case of brief quotations embodied in critical articles and reviews.

This book is a work of non-fiction. Unless otherwise noted, the author and the publisher make no explicit guarantees as to the accuracy of the information contained in this book and in some cases, names of people and places have been altered to protect their privacy.

WestBow Press books may be ordered through booksellers or by contacting:

WestBow Press
A Division of Thomas Nelson & Zondervan
1663 Liberty Drive
Bloomington, IN 47403
www.westbowpress.com
1 (866) 928-1240

Because of the dynamic nature of the Internet, any web addresses or links contained in this book may have changed since publication and may no longer be valid. The views expressed in this work are solely those of the author and do not necessarily reflect the views of the publisher, and the publisher hereby disclaims any responsibility for them.

Any people depicted in stock imagery provided by Getty Images are models, and such images are being used for illustrative purposes only.
Certain stock imagery © Getty Images.

ISBN: 978-1-9736-9094-8 (sc)
ISBN: 978-1-9736-9093-1 (hc)
ISBN: 978-1-9736-9095-5 (e)

Library of Congress Control Number: 2020907622

Print information available on the last page.

WestBow Press rev. date: 6/2/2020

Scriptures marked NIV are taken from the NEW INTERNATIONAL VERSION (NIV): Scripture taken from THE HOLY BIBLE, NEW INTERNATIONAL VERSION ®. Copyright©1973, 1978, 1984, 2011 by Biblica, Inc.™. Used by permission of Zondervan

Scriptures marked NKJV are taken from the NEW KING JAMES VERSION (NKJV): Scripture taken from the NEW KING JAMES VERSION®. Copyright© 1982 by Thomas Nelson, Inc. Used by permission. All rights reserved.

Scriptures marked KJV are taken from the KING JAMES VERSION (KJV): KING JAMES VERSION, public domain.

Scriptures marked ERV are taken from the Holy Bible: Easy-to-Read Version (ERV), International Edition © 2013, 2016 by Bible League International and used by permission.

Scriptures marked ESV are taken from THE HOLY BIBLE, ENGLISH STANDARD VERSION (ESV): Scriptures taken from THE HOLY BIBLE, ENGLISH STANDARD VERSION ® Copyright© 2001 by Crossway, a publishing ministry of Good News Publishers. Used by permission.

Scriptures marked NLT are taken from the HOLY BIBLE, NEW LIVING TRANSLATION (NLT): Scriptures taken from the HOLY BIBLE, NEW LIVING TRANSLATION, Copyright©1996, 2004, 2007 by Tyndale House Foundation. Used by permission of Tyndale House Publishers, Inc., Carol Stream, Illinois 60188. All rights reserved. Used by permission.

Scriptures marked NASB are taken from the NEW AMERICAN STANDARD BIBLE®, Copyright © 1960, 1962, 1963, 1968, 1971, 1972, 1973, 1975, 1977, 1995 by The Lockman Foundation. Used by permission.

Scripture quotations marked MSG are taken from THE MESSAGE, copyright © 1993, 2002, 2018 by Eugene H. Peterson. Used by permission of NavPress. All rights reserved. Represented by Tyndale House Publishers, Inc.

Scriptures marked CSB are taken from The Christian Standard Bible. Copyright © 2017 by Holman Bible Publishers. Used by permission. Christian Standard Bible®, and CSB® are federally registered trademarks of Holman Bible Publishers, all rights reserved.

CONTENTS

Dedication ix
Introduction: The Spirit versus the Flesh xi

SECTION I: GODWARD RELATIONSHIP

Chapter 1   The Fruit of Love 1
Chapter 2   The Fruit of Joy 16
Chapter 3   The Fruit of Peace 35

SECTION II: HUMANWARD RELATIONSHIP

Chapter 4   The Fruit of Patience 49
Chapter 5   The Fruit of Kindness 69
Chapter 6   The Fruit of Goodness 81

SECTION III: INWARD RELATIONSHIP

Chapter 7   The Fruit of Faithfulness 97
Chapter 8   The Fruit of Gentleness 116
Chapter 9   The Fruit of Self-Control 130

Conclusion 147

DEDICATION

I dedicate this book to God the Father, God the Son, God the Holy Spirit, and His people.

In my work, I've encountered seven different types of believers who all desire to incorporate God into every area of their lives, specifically as He relates to their work. They are all mission-driven individuals who are after God's heart, and I admire how they show up in Christ. Although I had seven individuals in mind specifically, I recognize there are many believers out there who can relate, which is why I dedicate this book to all those inspired to live and walk by the Spirit in every area of their lives, including their work.

We all have a significant role to play in the kingdom of God. With this being the case, there is no job outside of God's grace. We as believers must know that God wants to be a part of all our affairs. To ensure God is in them, we need to invite Him in. If you can relate, or see yourself as being one of the types of leaders mentioned below, I encourage you to abide in Christ and recognize that He is our example.

One Leadership Style: Servant
Seven Leadership Types

Type 1: Joyful leader—sees God in her work and connects the dots between her work and God's Word.

Type 2: Peaceful leader—looks for facts and tactical steps as to how to apply God's Word to her life.

Type 3: Patient leader—remembers God's Word and how the Holy Spirit connects every area of her life.

Type 4: Kind leader—confirms who God is and reaffirms that all he has is all he needs.

Type 5: Good leader—reminds himself of God's grace and uses God's Word to help others invite God in.

Type 6: Faithful leader—converses with God often about how to transform her thoughts in order to take significant steps.

Type 7: Gentle leader—excited about learning new perspectives regarding God's Word and making it practical.

Going to our foundational scripture, Galatians 5:22–23 (NASB), we read: "But the fruit of the Spirit is love, joy, peace, patience, kindness, goodness, faithfulness, gentleness, and self-control; against such things there is no law." These seven leadership types represent the fruit of the Spirit. They are the archetypes of a servant leader. You may wonder, *If that is true, why are there only seven and not nine? What about love and self-control?*

> Love and self-control come only from God. He is love, and the Holy Spirit is self-control. Although we may be one of the aforementioned leadership types, Jesus is our example. You cannot be a Spirit-led leader without God the Father, our love; God the Son (Jesus), our example; and God the Holy Spirit, our self-control. You need all three to be Spirit-led. Just as I came to this conclusion, I pray and trust the Holy Spirit will lead you to this conclusion.

INTRODUCTION
THE SPIRIT VERSUS THE FLESH

In Galatians 5:16–23 (NASB), the scripture states:

> But I say, walk by the Spirit, and you will not carry out the desire of the flesh. For the flesh sets its desire against the Spirit, and the Spirit against the flesh; for these are in opposition to one another, so that you may not do the things that you please. But if you are led by the Spirit, you are not under the Law. Now the deeds of the flesh are evident, which are: immorality, impurity, sensuality, idolatry, sorcery, enmities, strife, jealousy, outbursts of anger, disputes, dissensions, factions, envying, drunkenness, carousing, and things like these, of which I forewarn you, just as I have forewarned you, that those who practice such things will not inherit the kingdom of God. But the fruit of the Spirit is love, joy, peace, patience, kindness, goodness, faithfulness, gentleness, self-control; against such things there is no law.

I start with this scripture because it is the foundational truth of *The Spirit-Led Leader*, which is a spiritual book about business for which the Holy Spirit has inspired the writing. This book is not about religion. To clarify what I mean, let us explore the meaning of religion and spirit.

According to the *Merriam-Webster Dictionary*, religion is:

1. the service and worship of God or the supernatural;
2. commitment or devotion to religious faith or observance;
3. a personal set or institutionalized system of religious attitudes, beliefs, and practices; conscientiousness;
4. a cause, principle, or system of beliefs held to with ardor and faith.[1]

On the other hand, *spirit* is defined by the *Merriam-Webster Dictionary* as:

1. an animating or vital principle held to give life to physical organisms;
2. a supernatural being or essence;
3. temper or disposition of mind or outlook especially when vigorous or animated;
4. the immaterial intelligent or sentient part of a person;
5. the activating or essential principle influencing a person; an inclination, impulse, or tendency of a specified kind (mood);
6. a special attitude or frame of mind;
7. a lively or brisk quality in a person or a person's actions;
8. a person having a character or disposition of a specified nature;
9. *capitalized, Christian Science:* God.

What's important to understand is the commonality of the two words. They both require a system of beliefs. For religion, the common belief is that there is a higher being; meanwhile, spirit is the supernatural association with religion. However, notice that neither definition mentions the other word. For example, the definition of religion does not include the word *spirit*, and the definition of spirit does not include the word *religion*. Yet if I say a business leader should be spirit-led, society would say I have violated a social norm!

What I recognize is that it's not necessarily the spirit that is lacking but rather the type of spirit leading. So the question is, what spirit is leading you in the different areas of your life and the lives of those you lead? Is it a spirit of fear, anxiety, worry, the Holy Spirit?

---

[1] *Merriam-Webster Dictionary*, s.v. "religion," https://www.merriam-webster.com/dictionary/religion.

The place in which you struggle is the place in which you need to test your spirit. First John 4:1 (NASB) states, "Beloved, do not believe every spirit, but test the spirits to see whether they are from God, because many false prophets have gone out into the world." There is a warning about false prophets in Matthew 7:15–20 (NLT), which states:

> Beware of false prophets who come disguised as harmless sheep but are really vicious wolves. You can identify them by their fruit, that is, by the way they act. Can you pick grapes from thornbushes, or figs from thistles? A good tree produces good fruit, and a bad tree produces bad fruit. A good tree can't produce bad fruit, and a bad tree can't produce good fruit. So every tree that does not produce good fruit is chopped down and thrown into the fire. Yes, just as you can identify a tree by its fruit, so you can identify people by their actions.

No matter your religion, you are a spiritual being, and as such you are spirit-led. Now, you can't believe every spirit; you need to test the spirit continually. According to 2 Timothy 1:7 (NKJV), "For God has not given us a spirit of fear, but of power and of love and of a sound mind." This is an encouraging belief, whereas false prophets give a spirit of worry, fear, and anxiety—a limiting belief.

My point is that being spirit-led is an animating or vital principle held to give life to physical organisms. It is the essence, the outlook, the immaterial intelligence, or sentient part of a person. It is the activating or essential principle influencing a person. Talk about having a sense of urgency and being innovative! Spirit is the inclination, the impulse, the special attitude or frame of mind that limits or encourages forward movement. So, the takeaway?

1. We need to talk about being spirit-led at work.
2. We need to understand how we're leading.

What beliefs have shaped you into the person, manager, leader, or corporation you are today? Thinking of those beliefs, which of them are encouraging or limiting your growth?

To be Holy Spirit–led, which I will refer to with a capital "S" (i.e., Spirit-led), requires four elements:

1. faith
2. trust
3. grace
4. the Holy Spirit

These are the elements that allow you to live by the Spirit of God. When led by the Holy Spirit, you influence others with the fruit of the Spirit. The essence of being a Spirit-led leader is to walk in the Spirit of God. So a Spirit-led leader is to live by faith, trusting God, receiving His grace, and being drawn to salvation through the Holy Spirit. It is to walk in the Spirit by influencing people through the fruit of the Spirit—love, joy, peace, patience, kindness, goodness, faithfulness, gentleness, and self-control—so that they too may invite God into their lives. The critical takeaway: As a Spirit-led leader, you are influencing others while God is influencing you.

By producing the fruit of the Spirit, you are living by the Spirit and not by the flesh. Given this fact, you have a helper and advocate, the Holy Spirit, who is the power of God to help you perform in excellence. Recognizing your performance, you must note the direction given in Galatians 5:25 (NIV): "Since we live by the Spirit, let us keep in step with the Spirit." Notice it says "keep in step." This is to help you understand that you can live in the Spirit and outpace the Spirit because you've received grace. When the Holy Spirit is helping you perform, you may start to run to your next step, thereby getting out of step with God. Galatians 5:25 reminds us to stay in pace with God as it is His grace that enables us to be successful when we move forward.

Leaders are constantly striving for work-life balance, overlooking the fact that the two are in opposition to one another. The reality is, work-life is not a matter of balance; it is a matter of choice. Going back to the foundational scripture, Galatians 5:17 (CSB), we read, "For the flesh desires what is against the Spirit, and the Spirit desires what is against the flesh; these are opposed to each other so that you do not do what you want." To understand the correlation between work and life and the Spirit versus the flesh, let's see how the *Merriam-Webster Dictionary* defines *work* and *life* and see some of their synonyms and antonyms:

- **Work:** something produced or accomplished by effort, exertion, or exercise of skill
  Synonyms for work: effort, exertion, labor, grind, might
  Antonyms for work: ease, fluency, smoothness
- **Life:** the sequence of physical and mental experiences that make up the existence of an individual
  Synonyms for life: existence, being, living, heart, growth, soul
  Antonyms for life: dullness, death, indifference

If you reflect on the definitions of work and life, you see that the two things are opposed to one another as work is a matter of doing and, in contrast, life is a matter of being. According to Romans 8:6 (NKJV), "For to be carnally minded is death, but to be spiritually minded is life and peace." To be carnally minded refers to having a mind-set that desires the flesh. In the foundational scripture, Galatians 5:16–17 (CSB), we read, "I say then, walk by the Spirit and you will certainly not carry out the desires of the flesh. For the flesh desires what is against the Spirit, and the Spirit desires what is against the flesh; these are opposed to each other." Romans 8:13 (NKJV) states, "If you live according to the flesh you will die; but if by the Spirit you put to death the deeds of the body, you will live."

These scriptures are meant to show you that work is the outcome of the flesh and that life is the outcome of the Spirit. To strive for work-life balance is really to strive for flesh-spirit balance, which is in opposition.

Key takeaway: You must choose to be work-led or life-led.

If you are a leader feeling drained, defeated, and concerned instead of having energy, courage, and vigor, then you are experiencing the deeds of the flesh instead of the fruit of the Spirit.

My mission through coaching is to help leaders be Spirit-led. By helping them to understand their limiting beliefs, I can help them reframe their thoughts and restructure their beliefs to overcome stagnation in their growth process. My purpose is to help leaders and companies grow through their encouraging beliefs, understanding what has shaped them into the people or company they are today and helping them to find what they will need to believe in to promote life, energy, courage, and vigor in the future.

The chapters ahead will focus on the fruit of
the Spirit and how to lead with them.

SECTION I
GODWARD RELATIONSHIP

*Seek the Lord and His strength; seek
His presence continually!
—1 Chronicles 16:11 (ESV)*

CHAPTER 1

THE FRUIT OF LOVE

Love is patient, love is kind and is not jealous; love does not brag and is not arrogant, does not act unbecomingly; it does not seek its own, is not provoked, does not take into account a wrong suffered, does not rejoice in unrighteousness, but rejoices with the truth; bears all things, believes all things, hopes all things, endures all things.
—1 Corinthians 13:4–7 (NASB)

Chapter Introduction

> For through the Spirit we eagerly await by faith the righteousness for which we hope. For in Christ Jesus neither circumcision nor uncircumcision has any value. The only thing that counts is faith expressing itself through love. (Galatians 5:5–6 NIV)

This scripture tells us that we need the Holy Spirit to have a strong desire to wait (and anticipate) righteousness. It is the activation of our faith that allows us to stand still and know, which we express through love. Said differently: faith is contingent on love; it does not count without it.

So what is love? The scripture states,

> Love is patient, love is kind and is not jealous; love does not brag and is not arrogant, does not act unbecomingly; it does not seek its own, is not provoked, does not take into account a wrong suffered, does not rejoice in unrighteousness, but rejoices with the truth; bears all things, believes all things, hopes all things, endures all things. (1 Corinthians 13:4–7 NASB)

To live by the Spirit, we must "serve one another humbly in love. For the entire law is fulfilled in keeping this one command: 'love your neighbor as yourself'" (Galatians 5:13 NIV).

The fruit of the Spirit can only be produced by God, and it is essential to note that love is the first fruit as God loved us first. "For God so loved the world, that He gave His only begotten Son, that whoever believes in Him shall not perish, but have eternal life" (John 3:16 NASB). It is through love that all things matter to God.

> If I have the gift of prophecy, and know all mysteries and all knowledge; and if I have all faith, so as to remove mountains, but do not have love, I am nothing. And if I give all my possessions to feed the poor, and if I surrender my body to be burned, but do not have love, it profits me nothing. (1 Corinthians 13:2–3 NASB)

We are nothing and we profit nothing without love. Also, there is no law against the fruit of the Spirit. In Matthew 22:37–40 (NASB), Jesus says, "You shall love the Lord your God with all your heart, and with all your soul, and with all your mind. This is the great and foremost commandment. The second is like it, you shall love your neighbor as yourself. On these two commandments depend the whole law."

Now understanding the importance and excellence of love, we are left with two questions: (1) How do we honor the greatest commandment of loving God with all our heart, soul, and mind? (2) How do we accept the second-greatest commandment and love our neighbor as ourselves?

Turning to Deuteronomy 30:6 (NASB) for clarification on the question "How do we love God with all our heart, soul, and mind?" we find that the scripture states, "Moreover the Lord your God will circumcise your heart and the heart of your descendants, to love the Lord your God with all your heart and with all your soul, so that you may live."

To illustrate this point, think about a callus on your hand. It is a thick, hardened layer of dead skin that is unattractive. According to the Mayo Clinic, calluses are developed when your skin tries to protect itself against friction and pressure. They also say you only need treatment if the callus causes discomfort. For most people, eliminating the source of friction or pressure will make the callus disappear. To circumcise means to remove a layer of skin. As stated in Deuteronomy 30:6, God removes (circumcises) the layer of dead skin that was developed by the friction and pressure of this world, which created a toughness that hindered you from loving tenderly. By eliminating the source of your friction and pressure, God has given you a new heart—one that allows you to love Him with all your heart and all your soul so that you may live.

What about our minds? The scripture says:

> Because of the hardness of their heart; and they, having become callous, have given themselves over to sensuality for the practice of every kind of impurity with greediness. But you did not learn Christ in this way, if indeed you have heard Him and have been taught in Him, just as truth is in Jesus, that, in reference to your former manner of life, you lay aside the old self, which is being corrupted in accordance with the lusts of deceit, and that you be renewed in the spirit of your mind, and put on the new self, which in the likeness of God has been created in righteousness and holiness of the truth. (Ephesians 4:18–24 NASB)

The love of God is so incredible that He first sits with you to remove what is hardening your heart so that you may know Him, hear Him, and be taught by Him. By being in His presence, you lay aside your old self, full of lust (false love), and put on your new self in the likeness of God (love). The ability to do so is the result of being renewed in the spirit of your mind.

Remember that 2 Timothy 1:7 (NASB) says, "For God hath not given us the spirit of fear; but of power, and of love, and of a sound mind."

That known, God gives us the love He wants from us and the love He wants us to give to others. The love we show others is evidence of God's perfect love. Romans 12:2 (NASB) states, "Do not be conformed to this world, but be transformed by the renewing of your mind, so that you may prove what the will of God is, that which is good and acceptable and perfect."

Key takeaway: In order to be given God's love and to be able to love others, we must abide in God.

To abide means to live or dwell in. This is my interpretation of 1 John 4:16–17 (NASB): To dwell in love is to express love. Whoever shows love lives in God. By staying in love and in God, our love is perfected—which gives us confidence because as He is, so are we in this world.

Leading with Love—Jesus in Action

The scripture says God is love and that God loved us so much, He gave His one and only Son, Jesus, to save us. The Bible simply instructs us to love God first and love others second. So in leading with love, we are to love God first by abiding in Him and next by loving others in the way that we've grown to know love. First John 3:16 (NASB) says, "We know love by this, that He laid down His life for us; and we ought to lay down our lives for the brethren." The Bible says we're not to show love through words and communication but, instead, with actions and facts. This is interesting because when we think of someone we love, we wonder if we've told them we love them enough. We question whether we've communicated our love in a way that shows them just how much we love them. However, the Bible says that it's more about how we act around them than what we tell them. It's about being honest with them, telling them the truth rather than communicating in a way that doesn't hurt their feelings. So when we think about leading with love at work, it's not about telling people you love them or regularly communicating how much you love them. It's not about thinking you're protecting them by not sharing the truth about their performance or demeanor in fear you'll hurt their feelings. It's about how you act toward them and treat them. Your warmth, enthusiasm, concern, admiration (respect and approval), and honesty is love.

Although Jesus has not called you on the phone and said that He loves you, His actions show you that He does. He died for our sins over two thousand years ago. I would challenge you to think about what He has done for you lately, or better yet, what you would like for Him to do for you now. It could be life-changing or straightforward. I'll give you two examples of how Jesus shows up for me in a way that makes me smile: (1) When I have a deadline at work and have not finished the project, I pray and invite God into my situation. I acknowledge where I am and ask Him for help. Not long after I say *amen*, my meetings get canceled, clearing up my day to finish the project. The status meeting for the project gets rescheduled to a later time depending on how much time I need. Now some may not think this is a worthy miracle to praise God for; however, I know it is not by happenstance that the meetings get canceled. The time I get to finish the project is evidence of God's presence. (2) While I was writing *The Fruit of a Spirit-Led Leader*, my laptop went out, and I was on the verge of buying a new one to finish writing. The price of a new laptop, however, was not in my budget. I have a computer that is about five years old that's pretty beat up. My husband did a factory reset on it in preparation of tossing it out. Well, again, I invited God into this situation. After a few tries, I was able to get the computer set up and working like a brand-new one—at no cost to me. These perceived small acts were big for me, and although they weren't as life-changing as some of the other things God has done for me, they were the things I needed at the moment. As a bigger idea and takeaway, these acts let me know that God is present. No matter how big or small my problem, He leads me when I invite Him in.

Where has Jesus shown up for you? What has He done for you lately, and what would you like for Him to do for you now?

Since I am unable to know what all Jesus has done and is doing in your life right now, I want to help you understand what He has done. First Peter 2:24–25 (NASB) states: "He Himself bore our sins in His body on the cross so that we might die to sin and live to righteousness; for by His wounds you were healed. For you were continually straying like sheep, but now you have returned to the Shepherd and Guardian of your souls." Jesus endured our punishment and died on a cross for us to be saved and be allowed to have a relationship with God the Father. In Matthew 27:29–30 (NASB), the Bible says, "And after twisting together a crown of thorns, they put it on His head, and a reed in His right hand; and they knelt down before Him and mocked Him, saying, 'Hail, King of the Jews!' They spat on Him and took the reed and began to beat Him on the head." Jesus was betrayed, denied, mocked, spit on, beaten, charged for crimes He didn't commit, and finally killed so that we may have a chance at eternal life with God. To endure all of that as an innocent man without complaint, feeling that it was necessary for saving us, is an act of love. This isn't a sad story, however, because Jesus conquered death. In Matthew 28:17-20 (NASB), we read that upon seeing Jesus after His resurrection, they worshipped Him; but some were doubtful. They were given authority to make disciples of all the nations, baptizing them and teaching them. They had a knowing that He was always with them.

Now knowing Jesus's action, how people responded, and the impact of His works, how do you take what Jesus did as an example of how you can lead with love?

At work, a common phrase people use to describe being betrayed by someone they work closely with for their selfish gain is "thrown under the bus." This usually happens when someone you trust, a friend, puts your name out there when what is being discussed is controversial, unpopular, or inconvenient for them to deal with. If you think about Jesus's crucifixion, you see that it started with a friend's betrayal. Judas, a disciple, betrayed Jesus for thirty pieces of silver. In Matthew 26:48 (NASB), we read, "Now he who was betraying Him gave them a sign, saying, 'Whomever I kiss, He is the one; seize Him.'" Jesus's response appears in verse 50 of this chapter: "'Friend, do what you have come for.' Then they came and laid hands on Jesus and seized Him." Judas threw Jesus under the bus for his own personal gain—money (thirty pieces of silver). Now I wouldn't daresay that Judas's betraying Jesus is the same as your throwing your employee or friend under the bus for money. But my question to you is, how much different is it when in business we throw our friends under the bus to secure our job (i.e., keep our paycheck)? In essence, when you throw a colleague under the bus at work, you are betraying a friend for money (irrespective of the consequence).

Point #1. Don't be Judas at work.
Point #2. Respond like Jesus.

To ensure you're able to make those points tactical, here are a few principles to help. Regardless of the situation, of changes in your goals, or of top management requests, these principles will allow you to focus on God.

Guiding Principles:

1. Gather with your friends to inform them about what is happening in your life.
2. Keep the friends you can be vulnerable around (the ones you can cry in front of) closest to you.
3. Spend quiet time with God, expressing how you (really) feel about what you're going through.
4. Know your life is prophesied, so all that is taking place is according to God's purpose.
5. Remember Romans 8:28 (NASB): "God causes all things to work together for good to those who love God, to those who are called according to His purpose."

Note: All things working together for your good is contingent on your loving God. How do you ensure God knows that you love Him? Knowing what you know now, you acknowledge that love isn't merely a word or something you continually say. It requires action and truth, where the action is worship.

The *Merriam-Webster Dictionary* shows two entries for *worship*. The first entry is the verb form of *worship*: to regard with great or extravagant respect, honor, or devotion. Synonyms are *adore*, *cherish*, and *love*. Antonyms are *abominate*, *despise*, and *hate*. The second entry is the noun form of *worship*: extravagant respect or admiration for or devotion to an object of esteem. A synonym is *idolatry*. There are no antonyms.

To understand this fully, let's also define what a verb and a noun are. A verb is a word that shows action, occurrence, or state of being. A noun is a person, place, or thing to serve as the subject of a verb.

The difference between loving God (walking by the fruit of the Spirit) and idolizing people, places, or things (a deed of the flesh) is all in your worship.

Question: How are you worshipping? Is it an action, or is it done for a person, place, or thing?

The truth: God created us to worship. Jesus said in John 4:23 that God seeks worshippers. Your default is set to worship. Assess whether you are walking by the Spirit or by the flesh. Check in with yourself to assess whether your worship is the subject or the display of your action.

In Psalms 147:11 (CEV), we read, "The Lord is pleased only with those who worship Him and trust His love." Put slightly differently, the Lord is pleased only with those who show Him extravagant respect, honor, and devotion. This means that anything you do to show God respect, honor, and devotion with no reason or motive other than respecting, honoring, and devoting time to Him is an act of worship.

Our job is to please God. The Bible says it is impossible to please God without faith (Hebrews 11:6). Earlier in the chapter, we learned that faith is contingent on love. Faith is the substance of things hoped for and the evidence of things not seen (Hebrews 11:1 KJV). This requires us to trust what we're hearing from God by being in a relationship with Him and obeying what He says. David says in Psalms 69:30, 31 (NASB), "I will praise the name of God with song and magnify Him with thanksgiving. ...

It will please the Lord." And in Romans 8:8 (NASB), we read, "Those who are in the flesh cannot please God."

God is pleased with *only* those who worship Him, and to worship Him is to take action that pleases Him, so let's make it clear what we need to do.

1. Love God.
2. Have faith.
3. Trust God.
4. Be obedient.
5. Thank God.
6. Praise God.
7. Walk in the Spirit of God.

These actions please God, which makes them acts of worship, serving as a display of your love for God.

As a leader, you may not always recognize how you show up to work, and frequently you may have no one around to be honest with you about how you have shown up. However, when you come to work filled with the love of God because you are living a life of worship, your love overflows to those who encounter you. As stated in 1 Thessalonians 3:12 (NIV), "May the Lord, make your love increase and overflow for each other and for everyone else." Respecting your team, honoring their work, and devoting time to advise, coach, mentor, and teach them and care about their lives is an overflowing of your love toward God.

Personal Reflection

I was given a leadership role that entirely made me feel unqualified for the position. However, I felt that God would not have allowed me to get the job if it wasn't mines to have. Every morning before I went to work, I listened to a message and praised and worshipped God through prayer, thanksgiving, and songs until I felt excited and on fire for God. The energy was contagious in the office, and my productivity was supernatural. Being new to the company, the industry, and the role, I had a steep learning curve. I did not realize the amount of work I was doing or how much I was impressing those around me. It was the first time in my career that my workload increased while my efforts decreased. I was getting things done not by might and energy but by God's power. The days I didn't find time for worship, I felt like I was driving in the car with no seat belt on. I felt vulnerable, and although I felt covered, I didn't feel completely safe. From this experience, I recognized that when you are walking by the Spirit, people are going to compliment you continually, sending you praises to boost your confidence, but remember, it is the anointing, the fragrance of the fruit of the Spirit, that people around you are experiencing. During this time, it was vital for me to humble myself by remembering that I was at a competitive advantage. I had the Holy Spirit as a helper and advocate, guiding me. In Galatians 5:26 (NASB), we read, "Let us not become boastful, challenging one another, envying one another." I recognize why this scripture is so important; when you're being told how awesome and amazing you are, it's easy to forget God and give Him glory for the awesomeness. To keep myself in check, I take a few steps:

1. For every compliment someone sows into me, I plant it into someone else.
2. Find time to teach others what I know and coach them to improve in areas they want to improve.
3. Disengage with negative talk even when listening and shift the conversation to positive talk.

Aside from these three practical actions, I adopted a mind-set that saw that those compliments and praises were really for God. People weren't complimenting me; they were applauding the God in me. Without my daily time with God, my darkness would have shown instead of my light. Because of this, I accepted those compliments on behalf of God as validation that I had represented Him well. My daily worship allows me time with God to express my love for Him, which overflows into my day, allowing me to show my heart and to lead with love at work.

Key takeaway: For a leader, operating in love is an act of worship as it requires you to worship God, who then gives you the strength, confidence, and love you need to give to others.

Leading with love requires you to love God first and then to love others. To be a leader who operates in this fruit, you must spend time with God by getting in His presence, which is done through worship.

Action: Every morning, wake up before it's time for work and simply spend time with God. Learn about Him through reading the Bible, listening to sermons, or playing music. Praise Him by giving Him thanks for all He's done, is doing, and will do. Worship Him by acknowledging His role in your life and sharing how important He is to you. And pray to let Him know where you are and where you would like Him to help you be. Also ask Him for guidance and protection. Do this before doing anything else, and take notice of your day. What's different? How did you personally feel going into the office and throughout the day?

Leading with the Opposing Deed

Now that we know what it means to live and walk by love, it is essential to understand our flesh so that we're able to recognize when we're not living or walking in the Spirt. To recap, we learned that worship is what you must do to express your love to God. The synonym for worship is love, and the antonym is idolatry. Idolatry is a deed of the flesh, so recognize that depending on how you worship determines whether you are loving God or lusting for something else.

Often when we think of idols, we picture the golden calf or think of figures from other religions (such as the Hindu god Ganesh). However, I want to extend the definition so that you, too, may understand that as Christians we create idols and, if we're not careful, we worship those idols without knowing. So, what is an idol?

An idol, as defined by the *Merriam-Webster Dictionary*, is "an object of extreme devotion, a representation or symbol of an object of worship, a likeness of something, a false conception, form, or appearance visible without substance." This definition makes me translate the meaning as follows: Anything you devote an extreme amount of time to is an idol. The person, place, or thing you honor, admire, and love much is an idol. Anything you try to imitate is an idol. Anything you value that has no substance is an idol. The key to understanding this is knowing that anything you decide to love more than you love God is considered an idol. Remember that love is to show through actions and facts, so although you may not say you love your job, your deciding to work sixty to ninety or more hours per week shows that it is love and possibly taking you away from spending time with God.

We make idolatry a one-sided concept, judging the people in the story of Exodus 32 (the golden calf) and priding ourselves on not dancing around golden objects. However, we get excited about buying a car, and then we make an effort not to park near other vehicles for fear someone will potentially dent the car or chip the paint. Think of one of the things that makes your heart beat. Is it your children? Is it your spouse? Is it worry or fear? Is it ambition? Think about what you do that takes up most of your time. Now ask yourself if it is worthy of the time you devote to it. Is your time spent on these other things hindering your time with God? If you answer yes to that last question, then yes, it is an idol. The good news is that you can dethrone idols by recognizing your actions and the facts.

If you're spending an extreme amount of time doing or thinking about something, remember God and make room for Him. I tend to overwork myself. I get caught up in my things-to-do list and start feeling overwhelmed. There isn't enough time to do anything else outside of work, so I don't do those other things. As a result, I worry that I'm underqualified and in over my head and that I have too much to do with not enough time to do it. When this happens, I find that I have overpromised and underdelivered to my spouse, family, and friends, who now are disappointed and distant. When I'm in this cycle, I realize that I am driven by a spirit of worry. Worry is an indicator that we're not worshipping. Our attention is focused on what and how and not on God and what God is doing. I now check in with myself to recognize when I am walking in the flesh.

Check yourself. Get in God's presence and answer the following questions:

1. What are you currently making space for, and what are you not currently making space for?

2. What are you currently making time for, and what are you not currently making time for?
3. What are you prioritizing right now, and what are you not prioritizing?

Looking at your responses, ask yourself what the Holy Spirit is showing you.

Now decide: What would you like to prioritize, make space and time for? How will this allow you to focus and make room for God to appear in all you're doing?

Chapter Summary—Love in Essence

"Love is patient, love is kind and is not jealous; love does not brag and is not arrogant, does not act unbecomingly; it does not seek its own, is not provoked, does not take into account a wrong suffered, does not rejoice in unrighteousness, but rejoices with the truth; bears all things, believes all things, hopes all things, endures all things." And love can only be produced by God. Of the fruit of the Spirit, love is the first fruit as God loved us first, giving His only Son, Jesus, to die on a cross for our sins. It is through love that all things matter to God. We are nothing and profit nothing without love. Jesus said the two greatest commandments are to (1) love the Lord with all your heart, soul, and mind and (2) love your neighbor as yourself. To do this, you must abide in God. We read in 1 John 3:16 (NASB), "We know love by this, that He [Jesus] laid down His life for us." The scripture says that we're not to show love through words and communication but instead with actions and facts. Jesus's action was dying so that we might live. He endured our punishment so that we may have a relationship with God. At the time, His disciples were afraid and doubtful as witnesses to all that was happening. However, they had great joy and worshipped Him upon seeing His resurrection. Worship is our way of showing God that we love Him. As defined in the chapter, worship is love. As an action (verb), it means to regard with great extravagant respect, honor, or devotion. If worship is the person, place or thing (noun), then it is idolatry, which is a deed of the flesh and an indicator of not walking (or leading) by love. God is pleased with only those who worship Him, and to worship Him is to take action that pleases Him. Again, the following actions are necessary for pleasing God:

1. Love God.
2. Have faith.
3. Trust God.
4. Be obedient.
5. Thank God.
6. Praise God.
7. Walk in the Spirit of God.

For leaders, operating in love is an act of worship as it requires us to worship God, who then gives us the strength, confidence, and love we need to give to others. Leading with love requires us to love God first and then to love others. To be a leader operating in love, we must spend time with God by getting in His presence, which is done through worship. *Note:* If we're not careful, we may develop idols and start worshipping without much awareness. An idol can be anything (a person, place, or thing), so remember to get in God's presence to assess what you're making space for, finding time to do, and prioritizing.

Steps Forward

Outlined below are tactical steps you may take to allow the Holy Spirit to work and produce love in your life:

- **Identify** what emotion(s) describe how you now feel about love.
- **Identify** what triggered the emotion(s); write it down.
- **Think** of a time when you led with love. What triggered your action(s)?
- **Assess** what you're holding dear to your heart. Is it hindering you from spending time with God? If yes, pray for God to help you reprioritize Him to be your number one priority and give you time to worship Him first before doing anything else.
- **Identify** a scripture (choose one from the chapter or one that comes to mind through your study) that reminds you of God's love and how God's Holy Spirit produces love in your life.

THE FRUIT OF LOVE

- **Repeat** the scripture until it resonates and you have memorized it.
- **Quote** the scripture every time you feel as if you're valuing something more than God.
- **Write** what you're prioritizing over God and what you can do to reprioritize to make God first and all others secondary.
- **Pray** over what you wrote.
- **Thank God** for providing you with clarity and understanding on how to reprioritize the things getting in the way of your receiving and giving the love of God.

End-of-Chapter Activity

Use this time to self-reflect and understand how this information is relevant to your life. Spend time with God now to worship Him and invite Him in. Do this while answering the following questions:

1. How is love showing up in your work?
2. If you currently don't see how it does show up, how would you like for love to show up?
3. What can you do specifically to make time for God and prioritize spending time with Him each day?
4. What one tactical step are you willing to commit to taking every time you find yourself idolizing something?
5. What makes committing to this one step vital for you?

Closing Scripture

Jesus said, "If you keep My commandments, you will abide in My love; just as I have kept My Father's commandments and abide in His love. These things I have spoken to you so that My joy may be in you and that your joy may be made full" (John 15:10–11 NASB).

CHAPTER 2

THE FRUIT OF JOY

*For His anger is but for a moment, His favor is
for a lifetime; Weeping may last for the night,
but a shout of joy comes in the morning.*
—Psalms 30:5 (NASB)

Chapter Introduction

When we think of joy, most of us think of happiness. We use the two words interchangeably as we assume they mean the same thing. For some of us, we've grown to know this isn't true, understanding that joy is trusting that God will. This understanding allows us to display a posture of confidence and hope because we believe God no matter the situation. Happiness, on the other hand, is the settlement of joy because it continually changes with the situation or circumstances of life. This chapter will take a closer look at what joy is and how it is produced by the Holy Spirit. As a leader, you will get a better understanding of how to develop yourself with fear (not anxiety) and learn how to identify your focus and then refocus to retain your joy.

In Hebrews 12:1–2 (NLT), the scripture says, "Therefore, since we are surrounded by such a huge crowd of witnesses to the life of faith, let us strip off every weight that slows us down, especially the sin that so easily trips us up. And let us run with endurance the race God has set before us. We do this by keeping our eyes on Jesus, the champion who initiates and perfects our faith. Because of the joy awaiting Him, He endured the cross, disregarding its shame. Now He is seated in the place of honor beside God's throne." It is important to note that "because of the joy ... He endured the cross, disregarding its shame." This gives us an inclination of the power and definition of joy. Although Jesus felt God had forsaken Him at that moment, He stayed nailed to the cross regardless of the pain, the mockers, and the shame because He trusted God. This was the will of God, and because Jesus had a fixed focus on Him, He endured the cross instead of allowing pride and His ability to get off the cross to get in the way of God's will. Knowing the will of God brings you joy, "for God knows the plans for your life, plans to prosper you and not harm you, to give you hope and a future" (Jerimiah 29:11 NIV). To digest Hebrews 12:1–2 and understand what joy means, how joy feels, and how to have joy, let's look at the scripture in parts.

Part 1: Strip off every weight. To ensure we have the same definition of weight, note that in this scripture, it is used as a noun, which indicates a person, place, or thing. Think of every weight in the context of burden, pressure, and force. The scripture says to strip off everything that slows you down. How do you identify what's slowing you down? By identifying what's causing you hardship or distress (burden), what's stressing you out (pressure), and the person, place, or thing you're putting all your strength or might into (force). Often it's easy for us to comprehend a burden or pressure and then strip it off, but force is tricky. Force involves our striving to do something, to put forth effort in achieving or obtaining a thing. Culturally this may be what you've been taught to do. So, what's wrong with this? It's a weight. In Zechariah 4:6 (CSB), the Lord says, "Not by strength or by might, but by My Spirit." The Lord is telling us not to depend on ourselves using our own power and strength but to depend on His Holy Spirit. In this, remember 2 Corinthians 12:9 (NIV): "My grace is sufficient for you, for my power is made perfect in weakness." For the things you're striving for, reflect on what it would mean and look like for you to depend on God's power and might and not your own.

Part 2: Run with endurance by keeping our eyes on Jesus. In chapter 1, we discussed what it means to abide in Christ. Again, to ensure we're working off the same definition, let's define endurance. Endurance, according to the *Merriam-Webster Dictionary*, is "the ability to withstand hardship or adversity … to sustain a prolonged stressful effort or activity." This scripture states that to do such things, we must focus on Jesus. How do you focus on Jesus? Keep Him at the center of everything you do. To test whether God is at the center of every situation, ask yourself a few questions:

1. What are you eager to do, or what do you desire to complete?
2. What makes you impatient? If you had to name the reason, what would you say it is?
3. What have you fulfilled that you are delighted to have achieved?

For each question you answered, I imagine it brought you high anxiety and pride. We all have an answer to these questions; however, the harsh reality is they're I-centered and not God-centered. The reason you have anxiety is that you're exerting your might and not God's, so when you've put in blood, sweat, and tears, you're proud that you achieved what you were so eager to accomplish. At the same time, these things most likely "stole" your joy because during trouble, you had to overcome that trouble yourself. You had to finish what you'd started. The amazing grace of God is that what God starts, He will finish. His power is made perfect in your weakness, and knowing that alone is sufficient. When you feel anxious and prideful about anything, it is an indicator that you have taken your eyes off Jesus and that it is time to refocus on Him. That said, being joyful requires you to have a fixed focus.

Let's reflect for a moment. Think of a time at work that frustrated you to the point of anger. What about this situation angered you? Did you feel unnoticed or misunderstood? Did the objective or goal keep changing? Were there competing priorities? Did you have a sense you were the only one doing any real work or the hard work?

The truth of the matter is that when work angers us to the point that we're publicly complaining; feeling defeated, overwhelmed, overworked, and underappreciated; and questioning whether or not it's worth our effort, it's time to institute the "no complaining" rule and ask ourselves two questions:

1. How do I find pleasure in this particular situation?
2. How do I move from anger to pleasure?

The answer to both is that you fix your focus.

I know your anger is justified and your feelings are valid. However, if we look up the word *anger*, we find that the opposite meaning of the word is *pleasure*, which is a feeling of happy satisfaction and enjoyment (its synonym being *joy*). So, although you have every right to be angry, that particular situation makes you vulnerable by causing you to give away your joy. So as not to give in, you have to identify what about the situation specifically angered you. Then locate your focus. Once you know where you are, you can determine how to refocus. When I did this exercise, I realized my anger was caused by me. I had been focused on myself and how I felt, on my capabilities instead of God's. I had been trying to figure it out and find the answer instead of becoming the answer and being Spirit-led. I realized I had been trying where I needed to be trusting (God). So, to fix my focus, I needed to take "I" from the center of attention and place God back at the center and ask the questions that would lead me to serve others. Joy came at this moment because I realized I was working on something that did not have an answer. Trying to find the answer instead of becoming the answer was frustrating until I realized that shift.

For the situation you identified, do the following:

- Take a sheet of paper, and at the top of it write "Where's my focus?" Underneath that, make bullet points and write out all the things you're focused on. You can identify your focus by thinking through what about the situation made you angry. Invite the Holy Spirit into this exercise and allow Him to help identify your current focus.

- Once that is completed, beneath this section write, "How I need to refocus?" Same as above, make bullet points and write out what you should be focusing on instead.
- After completing both sections, reflect and gather your realization from the exercise.

Part 3: Because of joy, He endured the cross. Jesus was so focused on God, granting us the choice of eternal life, that He stayed to be defeated purposely. Why? He knew it was a temporary defeat. The pain at that moment was because His time had come. However, it was the joy of our being saved that allowed Him not to focus on the pain He felt in the moment. As stated in John 16:21 (NASB), "Whenever a woman is in labor, she has pain, because her hour has come; but when she gives birth to the child, she no longer remembers the anguish because of the joy that a child has been born into the world." What is the joy on the other side of the pain you need to endure right now? Rick Warren said, "The secret of endurance is to remember that your pain is temporary, but your reward will be eternal."[2] The reality is that you are going to face lots of problems and temptations with your joy being dependent on what you decide to focus on. If you choose to focus on the issue and not the solution, on the desire and not the development, then you'll give up. The key to focusing on joy is to endure what you're experiencing at the moment. It becomes essential then to develop endurance, which is done by not giving up.

Think of someone training for a marathon; that person has to build endurance. She runs each day, allowing herself to increase the number of miles she run over time. What you don't see is such a person going out and trying to run twenty-six miles for the first time ever, getting burnt out and giving up on the dream of completing the marathon. Instead, the person focuses on gradually increasing the number of miles she runs each day, enduring until the day of the marathon with the joy of overcoming something she thought she could never do. What it boils down to is that in order to endure, you must stay in the hardship by focusing on the joy presented on the other side of the hardship. According to James 1:2–4 (NASB), "Consider it all joy, my brethren, when you encounter various

---

[2] Rick Warren, *The Purpose-Driven Life* (Grand Rapids, MI: Zondervan, 2002).

trials, knowing that the testing of your faith produces endurance. And let endurance have its perfect result, so that you may be perfect and complete, lacking in nothing."

Part 4: Disregarding its shame. Let's for a moment put ourselves in Jesus's shoes to think about the shame He or those who believed in Him must have felt. Your manager has talked about how you are a fantastic leader, how you have come in and hit the ground running. The big project that needs to get done over the next few weeks should be given to you because he knows you'll be able to get started quickly and deliver results. Your family and friends are proud of you, sharing the good news about how you're working on this big project and how the extended responsibility is proof that you are top talent and trusted to deliver results making a significant impact on the company. You realize that the project will put a strain on you. You think to yourself of all the things you need to do to ensure its success and decide to put together a team to help you deliver the project. You and the team get started on the project and hit the first few milestones as planned, at which point everyone is giving you praises, patting you on the back, and cheering you on. Then it happens: you discover that someone on your team has made a colossal mistake that is going to push the timeline out because you have to fix that mistake.

You sit to figure out what needs to happen, which requires you to fire the person who made the mistake because he lied about what he did. You go to your manager and inform him of what happened. Instead of understanding, he bashes you for choosing the wrong person and for not correctly managing your team. He decides to tell the board that he is removing you as the leader of the project. Also, because of your lack of attention, he will demote you to a lesser position. You're hurt. Your family, friends, and team feel embarrassed. You know it wasn't your fault, and the shame of being demoted after being celebrated and promoted is unbearable.

How do you disregard this shame? Well, you decide what about the situation you will focus on. Will it be the failure; will it be what people are saying about you; or will it be the opportunity to endure? When on the cross, Jesus had a group of people mocking Him and a group of people supporting Him; however, He didn't acknowledge either. He stayed focused on the outcome of our salvation. Jesus could have focused on those who supported Him and on His feeling that He had let them down, and while in pain Himself, taken on the burden of failure. Or He could have focused on the mockers and how they felt His crucifixion had proven them right, that He wasn't enough to carry out the promise of God. But instead, He focused on God's will and ignored all that was happening around Him because both would have brought Him shame. Sometimes we need to have a narrow vision, focusing only on the light at the end of the tunnel, not worrying about whether we will be attacked or defeated while in the tunnel but focused on getting out of the dark and into the light.

Key Takeaways:

- Where your burden, pressure, and force are also lies your joy. It is your choice to have joy or to give it away, which all depends on what you decide to focus on.
- To have joy produced in your life, you must abide in Christ. Your connection to Him allows you to bear the fruit of joy. Jesus says in John 15:5 (NASB), "I am the vine, you are the branches; he who abides in Me and I in him, he bears much fruit, for apart from Me you can do nothing." In John 15:10–11 (NASB), Jesus goes on to say, "If you keep My commandments, you will abide in My love; just as I have kept My Father's commandments and abide in His love. These things I have spoken to you so that My joy may be in you and that your joy may be made full."

Leading with Joy—Jesus in Action

It is essential to start this section with the fact that Jesus was anointed with joy and holds more joy than anyone else. In Hebrews 1:9 (NIV) the Word says, "You have loved righteousness and hated wickedness; therefore God, your God, has set you above your companions by anointing you with the oil of joy." Because of the joy Jesus has, your being in His presence causes you to leap for joy in the same way John the Baptist leaped in Elizabeth's womb (Luke 1:41).

To understand how we can get that same kind of leaping joy, let's break down Luke 1:41–45 (NIV): "When Elizabeth heard Mary's greeting, the baby leaped in her womb, and Elizabeth was filled with the Holy Spirit. In a loud voice, she exclaimed: 'Blessed, are you among women, and blessed is the child you will bear! But why am I so favored that the mother of my Lord should come to me? As soon as the sound of your greeting reached my ears, the baby in my womb leaped for joy. Blessed is she who has believed that the Lord would fulfill His promises to her!'"

By being in Jesus's presence, you are privy to joy, which the Holy Spirit reveals. This revelation allows you to interpret what has happened or is happening. First, Mary (a vessel of God—carrying Jesus inside of her) spoke. Then the baby inside of Elizabeth leaped for joy (internal reaction). Lastly Elizabeth, overwhelmed with joy, interpreted what happened and concluded why it had happened.

Point #1. To access joy, you must be in the presence of the Lord, and then your joy will overflow.
Point #2. When a vessel of God speaks to you, what's within you will leap for joy.
Point #3. You are filled with the Holy Spirit, reacting with gladness, declaring what happened. You question why you're so favored, then interpret what you heard and what you felt inside, knowing you are blessed because you believed the Lord would fulfill His promises.

If this is the order of operation, the question remains, in what way can we lead with joy?

Let's take a closer look at what it means to be a vessel. According to the *Merriam-Webster Dictionary*, a vessel is a container for holding something or a person into whom some quality (such as grace) is infused. In Romans 9:21 (ESV), we read, "Has the potter no right over the clay, to make out of the same lump one vessel for honorable use and another for dishonorable use?" And 2 Timothy 2:21 (ESV) states, "Therefore, if anyone cleanses himself from what is dishonorable, he will be a vessel for honorable use, set apart as holy, useful to the master of the house, ready for every good work." God created each of us to be a vessel to contain what He has put inside of us. The moment you focus on doing the honorable things, God uses you to be a vessel and perform His good work. Being a vessel requires faith, the faith to believe what Jesus said in John 14:26 (NASB): "But the Helper, the Holy Spirit, whom the Father will send in My name, He will teach you all things, and bring to your remembrance all that I said to you." This is how you lead with joy, by being a vessel and knowing that you are blessed to be a blessing to others. In 2 Corinthians 4:7–9 (NASB) we find, "But we have this treasure in earthen vessels, so that the surpassing greatness of the power will be of God and not from ourselves; we are afflicted in every way, but not crushed; perplexed, but not despairing; persecuted, but not forsaken; struck down, but not destroyed." Remember this when things get tough or feel shameful, frustrating, and challenging to endure. The joy comes in knowing we are afflicted in every way. Still, choosing to stay focused on God's surpassing power, we can crush it and bear the pain of it and, not having been forgotten, overcome the destruction. God is bigger than our circumstances. We can look past what we see because it is temporary. As we read in 2 Corinthians 4:18 (NASB), "While we look not at the things which are seen, but at the things which are not seen; for the things which are seen are temporal, but the things which are not seen are eternal."

Jesus encompasses joy. That said, He is Joy, so His leading was with joy. Jesus says in John 15:5–11 (NIV):

> I am the vine; you are the branches. If you remain in me and I in you, you will bear much fruit; apart from me, you can do nothing. If you do not remain in me, you are like a branch that is thrown away and withers; such branches are picked up, thrown into the fire and burned. If you remain in me and my words remain in you, ask whatever you wish, and it will be done for you. This is to my Father's glory, that you bear much fruit, showing yourselves to be

my disciples ... I have told you this so that my joy may be in you and that your joy may be complete.

What is Jesus instructing you to do in this scripture?

1. Remain in Him.
2. Ask whatever you wish.
3. Bear much fruit.

How do you remain in Him? You consume His Word. When you stay in Him and when His Word remains in you, whatever you ask will be done. When what's being done is for the glory of God, you will bear much fruit, representing love, joy, peace, patience, kindness, goodness, faithfulness, gentleness, and self-control. When you bear much fruit, you're displaying the fruit of the Spirit and showing yourself to be a follower of Jesus. When you do these things, you receive Jesus's joy, which makes your joy complete. Without Jesus, your joy is incomplete. With incomplete joy, it is impossible to endure anything. You need Jesus to endure. Without Him and His Word, the best feeling accessible to you is happiness, which is temporal—something you can see. Your happiness is contingent on a circumstance or situation. When that circumstance or situation changes, so does your happiness. Don't settle for a temporal and incomplete state of joy when you can have a source of constant and complete joy.

In Luke 10 1–21 (NIV), Jesus sends out seventy-two ahead of Him to do His work. In the story, Jesus appointed the seventy-two, told them what to expect ("the harvest is plentiful, but the workers are few"), and sent them out. He told them to go, and He informed them how they would feel ("like lambs among wolves"), but He said they should take comfort in knowing that He was sending them. Jesus shared with them what to do and what not to do, what to say, and what they deserved. He confirmed their authority (telling them, "Whoever listens to you, listens to Me [God]; whoever rejects you, rejects Me; and whoever rejects Me, rejects who sent Me"). The seventy-two followed what Jesus said and came back with joy. Jesus made sure the seventy-two understood why they felt so much joy—because He had given them authority to overcome all the power of the enemy and made it so that nothing would harm them. He also corrected them on what they thought was worthy of rejoicing over and revealed to them what they should really be celebrating. At that moment, the Holy Spirit filled Jesus with joy and He said: "I praise You, Father, because for this is what You were pleased to do."

Point #1. Inform your people.
Point #2. Correct your people.
Point #3. Praise God.

To ensure you're able to lead with joy, incorporate the following few principles, which will help you guide your direct reports in such a way that they can endure the work you have set for them, which brings them joy and returns joy to you.

Guiding Principles:

1. **Prepare and inform.** Be clear, concise, and specific about whom you want to do the work, what they should expect while doing the job, and how they should handle certain things as they come up.
2. **Confirm and reassure.** Tell your employees to go and make sure they know that the work you're giving them is on your behalf. They should know that they are an extension of you; for those who encounter them, it is the equivalent of encountering you. If others reject those you lead, then they're rejecting you.
3. **Get validation.** Have your employees to report back about how the work made them feel. It should always bring them joy and as a result bring you joy (if it doesn't, assess what was lacking, such as preparation, information, confirmation, or reassurance).
4. **Correct misplaced joy.** Reveal to them what they don't know, and make sure they're rejoicing over the right things.
5. **Give God glory.** In the following way, say, "I praise you, Father, because _____, and acknowledge Your works as this is what You were pleased to do."

As a leader, you need to be specific and clear about what you are asking your people to do. Make sure they are well-informed and are aware of what to expect and what they deserve. Give them the confidence that knowing they can do the work set in front of them because you have asked them to do it on your behalf. When you do these things, you are imparting joy as your employees feel prepared, informed, confirmed, and reassured that they can do (endure) what's ahead of them. A team with joy brings you joy. It is critical, however, to remember that the only way to impart joy is by being connected to Jesus and remaining in His Word—as Jesus is the vine and we are the branches.

Key takeaway: Joy is generated only by Jesus. To impart joy to others, you must stay connected to Him by remaining in His Word. By doing so, your joy will be made full through the power of the Holy Spirit and overflow, allowing you to bear much fruit.

Personal Reflection

Psalms 1:1–3 (NLT) says, "Oh, the joys of those who do not follow the advice of the wicked, or stand around with sinners or join in with the mockers. But they delight in the law of the Lord meditating on it day and night. They are like trees planted along the riverbank, bearing fruit each season. Their leaves never wither, and they prosper in all they do."

Every morning, I wake up at 5:00 to spend time with God. During this time, I pray, listen to a message or read the Bible, listen to gospel songs, and take notes on what I receive from the Holy Spirit. Sometimes I lose track of time because of God's presence, and the feeling is overwhelmingly amazing. This time changes the entire trajectory of my day, making me more productive, sharp, and guided. When I shorten my time or fail to wake up to have enough time to do all these things, I feel like I am driving a car without a seat belt on. I feel covered, however vulnerable and insecure. I also tend to be my best self in the mornings, so sometimes if I have too much to do, I think, *Well, I'll wake up at 5:00 a.m. to pray. I'll skip devotion, praise, and worship and start on the thing I need to work on.* Every time I think this, I don't have enough time to complete that thing. It becomes a downward spiral with me worrying about how my day is going to go and being anxious about how best to spend the rest of my day. To say the least, I always come up short on days like these.

When I was working on a project that was drastically undermanaged, the simple task of creating a tracker for executive reporting and a centralized repository to house the data was a huge undertaking requiring more effort than either I or the manager could have imagined. For three months, I worked to learn the issues and how to streamline the process across eleven businesses to provide visibility to the senior leadership team. I was feeling good about what I had; the tracker and reports looked great, and others could look at the tracker and see that some real thought went into it. I set up a time with my manager to discuss the status of the project.

To be honest, it was a meeting for me to say, "Here is *all* the work I've done. I have a few things to tighten up, but I think we'll be able to roll this out to the teams in the next two weeks." My manager's initial reaction was "Wow, this is really great work." He then went on to say, "In addition to what you have, you should add a customer-specific analysis so we can go deeper on a particular customer. Also, add this to make it dynamic reporting to evolve this summary even further." To say I was upset is an understatement. I was flat-out angry, feeling like I'd created something that didn't exist and was hard to get. I'd put forth all this effort only now to feel like it was all for nothing. As I was listening to all the changes my manager claimed I needed to make, all I could think was, *you're trying to change what I've done before fully understanding why I did it. Over the past three months, I've been tracking to what we agreed initially was the goal, only for it to be changed at the finish line.* I felt frustrated and annoyed by the fact that I had provided something out of nothing and all my manager could focus on was my providing more. On top of this, I was up against competing priorities. I tried communicating this to my manager, only for him to say, "Welcome to my world." Here I was trying to work in excellence but being held back because I had more on my plate than I had time to handle, all while feeling disappointed and angry. I was upset at the fact that I had allowed this situation to develop in such a way that I reacted out of my flesh instead of my spirit. This was the moment I realized that no matter how much I was in the Word and trying to walk by the Spirit, I *still* reacted out of my flesh.

I went back to Galatians 5:16–23, recognizing that the emotion I was feeling was anger. So what's the opposite of that? Is it love, joy, kindness ...? That's when I decided to define the word *anger*, which is described as "a strong feeling of annoyance, displeasure, or hostility." Its antonyms are *pleasure* and *good humor*. I looked up the word *pleasure*, which is defined as "a feeling of happy satisfaction and enjoyment." Synonyms are *happiness, delight, joy, gladness, glee, satisfaction, gratification, contentment, enjoyment,* and *amusement*. This led me to the conclusion that the opposite of anger (a deed of the flesh) is joy (a fruit of the Spirit). I asked myself two questions: (1) How do I find pleasure in this particular situation? (2) How do I shift my feeling of anger to joy? As part of this discovery, I read an article by Larry Osbourne, a pastor in Vista, California, called "Leading with Joy." In it Osbourne talks about a situation that angered him, making him feel defeated, overwhelmed, and underappreciated and causing him to question whether the work he was doing was worth it—the exact feelings I had. He said that when you're a leader and feel angry so strongly that you openly complain about feeling defeated, overworked, and underappreciated, you must institute a "no complaining" rule. When you think this way, you remember that (1) leadership is a choice, (2) servant leadership requires you to be treated like a servant, (3) your reward comes from God, and (4) this temporary suffering is your opportunity to work more closely with God.

Now you may wonder how this story connects back to my morning ritual. Well, while I was doing the work of the project, I was spending time with God consistently. The morning I presented to my manager, I had cut my time short with God to prepare for the meeting, which turned into a total flop. It wasn't until going through the situation that I realized the reason I'd gotten so angry in the first place was that I was outpacing God's grace and trying to handle things myself. I was more focused on how *I* was feeling instead of how *God* was using this situation to develop me and establish my growth as a leader.

Key Takeaways:

1. Your time commitment to God is sacred. Whenever you decide to have it, and however long you decide to make it, God will always show up, so don't stand Him up.
2. When you shorten your time with God, you're the only one who comes up short.
3. It's not all those times before when you were in the Word that count; it's having the Word you need for today that counts. As we read in Isaiah 43:18 (NIV), "Forget the former things; do not dwell on the past."
4. You need the Word daily to operate in the Spirit, so meditate on it day and night. This unlocks your joy.

Leading with the Opposing Deed

I discovered that anger is the opposing deed to joy, a fruit of the Spirit. Recognizing this is important because as a leader you will find that some people and situations will provoke your anger, and you must understand how to handle moments like these. It is unrealistic to say or think you'll never get angry. After all, there will be times when your anger is justified. However, you must be able to shift that anger by removing your focus from I, them, or that and fixing it on God, which in turn will bring you joy.

In my personal reflection, I shared a story to illustrate how I felt and the questions I asked myself to make the shift. But I think it is imperative that I also share with you the two questions I asked myself to determine what I was focused on and how I fixed my focus, which, as a result, brought me joy.

Question 1: Where's my focus?

1. I am focused on finishing.
2. I am focused on not being seen as the one behind.
3. I am focused on avoiding project status updates and testing.
4. I am focused on not having to ask for help.
5. I am focused on when I said I would be done.

6. I am focused on being in the exact place I was (again).
7. I am focused on failing with a sense of, "If I don't figure this out, then *Oh man!*"
8. I am focused on the other tasks I haven't finished.
9. I am focused on everything else I'm not doing and, as a result, what I'll have to do.
10. I am focused on the task and problem (what I have to do) instead of the opportunity.

Question 2: How do I need to refocus?

1. Focus on God, recognizing I have a helper.
2. Focus on what I'm learning and how that's serving me.
3. Focus on how I don't have to do anything, that God has placed me and positioned me here to grow.
4. Focus on the purpose of the exercise.
5. Focus on the solution and how my thoughtfulness will serve the team.
6. Focus on having an opportunity to work on something needed that can be leveraged.
7. Focus on knowing where I stand with the project and writing out the questions that need answers.
8. Focus on being in God's presence.

Realization: I'd been trying where I needed to be *trusting*. I had been focused on me and how I felt, on my capabilities instead of God's. I had been trying to figure it out and find the answer instead of becoming the answer and being Spirit-led. I decided to focus on becoming the answer and start asking the questions I needed to ask to serve others! Being a servant leader requires you to serve.

Now go back to the exercise presented earlier in the chapter. Think of something at work that frustrated you to the point of anger. What about this situation angered you? Did you feel unnoticed or misunderstood? Did the objective or goal keep changing? Were there competing priorities? Did you feel as though you were the only one doing any real work or the hard work?

Ask yourself these two questions:

1. How do I find pleasure in this particular situation?
2. How do I move from anger to pleasure?

For the situation you identified, do the following:

- Take a sheet of paper. At the top of it write, "Where's my focus?" and underneath that, make bullet points, writing out all the things you're focused on. You can identify your focus by thinking of what about the situation made you angry. Invite the Holy Spirit into this exercise and allow Him to help identify your current focus.
- Once this is completed, beneath that write, "How I need to refocus?" and—same as above—make bullet points, writing out what you should be focusing on instead.
- After completing both sections, reflect and gather your realization from the exercise.

Chapter Summary—Joy in Essence

Remember, Jesus endured the cross because joy awaited Him. Joy is a powerful tool. It's something that brings you knowledge and understanding. Joy requires you to react, respond, and think in the Spirit. Without the Holy Spirit producing it, you will only experience happiness. What's great about having joy is that it's also about having perspective. Your perspective either unleashes your joy or ties it up, making it critical for you to be aware of your view. Joy is tactical in that there are a few actions you can take to access it always:

1. Strip off every weight.
2. Fix your focus on God.
3. Know that anger or pain is temporary.
4. Have tunnel vision.

Jesus reminds us that He is the vine and we are the branches, indicating that He is our source and that if we are to produce any fruit, we must stay connected to Him. To remain in Him requires us to remain in His Word, on which we should meditate day and night. As leaders, we are positioned to be vessels of God, to impart the fruit of the Spirit to others. That said, we must bear much fruit and be like a tree planted by the riverbank, bearing fruit in each season with leaves that never wither, and prospering in all we do (Psalms 1:3). Jesus wants to be able to help us in all we do, and the key to this is that when you invite Him in, you're allowing Him control to do just that. This partnership enables you to trust God and, in any circumstance, to bring you joy because He is the missing piece to make your joy full and complete.

Steps Forward

Think about how to apply what you've learned. Outlined below are tactical steps you may take to allow the Holy Spirit to work and produce joy in your life:

- **Identify** a situation(s) that describe how you now feel about joy.
- **Identify** what triggered your emotion of joy.
- **Think** of a time when you led with joy. What triggered your action(s)?
- **Assess** what you're focusing on. Is it hindering you from putting God at the center of your situation? If yes, pray for God to help you refocus in a way that allows Him to be in control.
- **Identify** a scripture (choose one from the chapter or one that comes to mind through your study) that reminds you of the joy God gives and how God's Holy Spirit produces joy in your life.
- **Repeat** the scripture until it resonates and you have memorized it.
- **Quote** the scripture every time you feel as if you're focusing on something more than you're focusing on God.
- **Write** what you are giving more attention to above what you're giving to God and what you can do to refocus, making God first and all else secondary.

- **Pray** over what you wrote.
- **Thank God** for providing you with clarity and understanding regarding how to refocus your attention and receive complete joy in all things you face.

End-of-Chapter Activity

Use this time to self-reflect and understand how this information is relevant to your life. Spend time with God now to worship Him, and invite Him in while you complete the following questions:

1. How are you finding joy in the work you currently do?
2. If you currently don't have any joy, what about your work is stealing your joy?
3. What can you do specifically to make time for God and prioritize spending time with Him each day?
4. What one tactical step are you willing to commit to taking to shift your focus every time you find yourself angry, sad, frustrated, or discouraged about something?
5. What makes committing to this one step essential for you?

Closing Scripture

"Deceit is in the hearts of those who plot evil, but those who promote peace have joy" (Proverbs 12:20 NIV).

CHAPTER 3

THE FRUIT OF PEACE

*Peace I leave with you; My peace I give to you;
not as the world gives do I give to you. Do not let
your heart be troubled, nor let it be fearful.*
John 14:27 (NASB)

Chapter Introduction

"For you will go out with joy and be led forth with peace" (Isaiah 55:12 NASB). Peace and joy are intertwined, yet they are different because it is possible to have both. Sometimes we describe the feeling of both in the same way as we say we have peace when indeed we may be experiencing joy. Oftentimes if we have joy, we're also at peace with whatever situation is putting our joy at risk. It is possible to experience peace without joy. This is the physical element (not the feeling). "My peace I give you" indicates that peace can be given and not only experienced as a feeling. Think of things like a peace treaty, freedom from something, or a state of security. This kind of peace you can see, and/or you can identify who or what has given you peace. However, as it relates to this chapter, we will focus on emotional peace. All references going forward will describe the feeling of peace. We will discuss how to know you have peace, how to produce the fruit of peace, and how God leaves His peace with you.

What is peace? Peace is a covenant between God and His people. In Ezekiel 34:25–30, God describes this covenant. His covenant promises safety, blessings, and prosperity. Paraphrased, God says that He will rid the land of savage beasts so you may live and sleep in safety. He will make you and the things surrounding you blessed. He will send down showers of blessings in season. The trees will yield their fruit and the ground its crops. You will secure the land. The Lord also mentions that you will know Him when He breaks you from bondage and rescues you from those who enslaved you. You will no longer be prey or the devoured. You will live in safety, and no one will make you afraid. He will provide a land renowned for its crops, and you will no longer be a victim of famine or insults. Then the Lord says, "You will know I'm with you and that you are My people." We are His people, which means God made this covenant with you and me. He wanted us to feel secure in knowing that we are safe, blessed, and prosperous. He also wanted us to understand how to identify Him and know Him. In doing that, we will be set free from whatever is keeping us bound. Internally, you will feel rescued and unafraid when you accept God's peace. You won't have to worry about starving or the insults of others, as neither will kill you.

God took the time to let us know what to expect and how to know Him and recognize He is with us. In Isaiah 54:10 (NIV), God says, "Though the mountains be shaken and the hills be removed, yet my unfailing love for you will not be shaken, nor my covenant of peace be removed." This covenant is ours. No matter what we're experiencing, no matter how difficult it gets, God wants us to know His covenant still applies. That means your peace comes from knowing God's promise. And in knowing God's promise, you "don't worry about anything; instead, pray about everything. Tell God what you need and thank Him for all He has done. Then you will experience God's peace, which exceeds anything we can understand. His peace will guard your hearts and minds as you live in Christ Jesus" (Philippians 4:6–7 (NLT). If this describes what peace is, how it makes us feel, and how God gives it to us, then how do we maintain or keep this peace?

Isaiah 26:3 (NLT) states, "You will keep in perfect peace, all who trusts you [the Lord], all whose thoughts are fixed on you [Lord]!" Once again, it is important to fix our thoughts on the Lord. When we abide in the

Lord, keeping our focus and thoughts on God, we maintain a perfect peace (experiencing love, joy, and peace).

Leading with Peace—Jesus in Action

God's peace comes through Jesus. In Ephesians 2:14–18 (NIV), we read,

> For He Himself [Jesus] is our peace, who has made the two groups one and has destroyed the barrier, the dividing wall of hostility, by setting aside in His flesh the law with its commands and regulations. His purpose was to create in Himself one new humanity out of the two, thus making peace, and in one body to reconcile both of them to God through the cross, by which He put to death their hostility. He came and preached peace to you who were far away and peace to those who were near. For through Him we both have access to the Father by the [Holy] Spirit.

In this scripture, we learn that Jesus is our peace, which indicates that if we don't have Jesus, we don't have peace. The scripture also reveals to us the outcome and purpose of Jesus's crucifixion.

Point #1. Our sins were crucified in His body, allowing us to have a relationship with God.
Point #2. Jesus's crucifixion made peace between God and mankind because Jesus (a man of no sin) died for us to give us access to God the Father through the Holy Spirit.

Key takeaway: Jesus is peace, Jesus preached peace, and Jesus made peace.

Now the question still remains, what can we do specifically to have peace? To better answer this question, it is essential that we first recognize when we need peace. When we think back on Galatians 5:16–22, we see that this scripture outlines the deeds of the flesh and the fruit of the Spirit. There are two deeds, strife (discord) and dissensions, which means struggle and disagreements—conflict. You need peace whenever you find yourself struggling, or having disagreements, or being in conflict or at war with someone or something. During these times, you need to invite Jesus in. In Matthew 11:28–29 (ERV), Jesus says, "Come to me all of you who are tired from the heavy burden you have been forced to carry. I will give you rest. Accept my teaching. Learn from me. I am gentle and humble in spirit. And you will be able to get some rest."

What is Jesus instructing us to do in this scripture?

1. Go to Him.
2. Accept His teachings.
3. Learn from Him.

For us to have peace, we must take what's worrying us, making us afraid, and causing us to struggle to Jesus. Allowing Him to take on our burdens, fears, and anxieties, we accept His teachings and learn from Him, being our example. When we do this, we will have peace.

As I started to think through examples of Jesus leading with peace, I noticed I couldn't find a story of Him per se leading with peace, although I could find a story with Him simply being peace. His being is the example of peace as He is the Prince of Peace. We read the following in Matthew 4:37–41 (NKJV):

> And a great windstorm arose, and the waves beat into the boat so that it was already filling. But He was in the stern, asleep on a pillow. And they awoke Him and said to Him, "Teacher, do You not care that we are perishing?" Then He arose and rebuked the wind and said to the sea, "Peace, be still!" And the wind ceased, and there was a great calm. But He said to them, "Why are you so fearful? How is it that you have no faith?" And they feared exceedingly, and said to one another, "Who can this be, that even the wind and the sea obey Him!"

This scripture is interesting because it illustrates that Jesus was already with His apostles; they didn't have to find Him. However, still in His presence, they became afraid and worried about the storm surrounding them. Jesus rebuked the wind and said, "Peace, be still," and then the wind ceased and there was a great calm. Jesus asked why His apostles were so afraid and why they questioned their faith. When you are already with Jesus, you don't have to go to Him, and if you have the faith to accept His teaching and learn from His Word, you will have peace. The storm distracted the apostles. It made them feel like (1) Jesus was there but asleep and had no understanding of what was going on around them and (2) the intensity of the storm was going to kill them. In Romans 5:1–2 (NKJV), we read, "Therefore, having been justified by faith, we have peace with God through our Lord Jesus Christ, through whom also we have access by faith into this grace in which we stand, and rejoice in hope of the glory of God." To have peace, you must have enough faith to believe you have access to Jesus. In John 16:32–33 (NKJV), Jesus tells us there will be times when we feel alone and experience tribulations. Still, we're not alone, and we must be of good cheer because He has overcome the world. Jesus told us this so that we may have peace. Accepting this and learning from Matthew 4:37–41, we shall have peace no matter what storm we're facing because we have the faith that Jesus is with us and that His Word, which we can accept and learn from, is true. And just like the disciples in the boat, we will be in awe of the level of peace as we feel "a great calm" as it relates to the storm in our lives. Don't be moved by what you see. Be moved by what you believe!

Guiding Principles:

1. **Get in God's presence.** Understand that peace only comes from the Lord. Being in His presence is required. However, it is important to know He is always there just waiting for you to invite Him in. You don't need to inform Him; you just need to involve Him.
2. **Have faith.** Don't be moved by the situation that is causing you conflict, as faith is the substance of things hoped for and the evidence of things not seen. Trust God's Word and remember Philippians 4:6–7 (paraphrased): Don't worry about anything, but in *all* things give it to the Lord.

3. **Receive peace.** Stop looking for peace and, instead, receive peace. You already have access to it and know how and where to go get it. You must recognize that your peace isn't lost or misplaced. It's available to you always because Jesus is available to you forever. So involve Him, accept Him, learn from Him, and receive His peace.

As a leader, you must stay calm and not overreact to any news you receive because your team is watching to see how they should react. You are their example, and if you're stressed, depending on how you handle it, you'll push that stress onto your team. What frequently happens is that your worries become their worries; your tribulations become theirs. Whether you like it or not, your responsibility as a leader is to be at peace, not moved by the trouble that comes your way. You must display a level of faith and expertise to your team that this too shall pass, all will work out. Without the reassurance that it will all work out, you stress over trying to have it all together, fearing that if you make the wrong decision or do the wrong thing, it will negatively impact your team and their families—this while also feeling unable to handle or control the situation you're facing. So what do you do? You get in God's presence, have faith, and know that this problem won't kill you but will serve as a platform for God to perform a miracle and provide a solution. This is where your peace comes from, knowing that God is with you and that all things work for the good of those who love the Lord.

Key takeaway: Peace is a way of being. It's knowing that God has got it all under control. And when you involve Him and have the faith to believe He's taking on your burden, you will have peace.

Personal Reflection

I had the honor to make history at a Fortune 10 company. I was the first to be accepted to an executive leadership development program without completing the foundational leadership development program. So when I joined the executive program, all eyes were on me with people assessing how well I'd do and *if* I'd be able to finish the program successfully. Although the offer felt like a blessing, the job felt like a burden, one that kept me worried, stressed, anxious, afraid, and lacking in confidence. However, through the experience, I had an entirely different encounter with God. It was through this program that I developed my relationship with God (and what I claim to be the real reason I was accepted). The program was structured in such a way that after two years, you make a choice on whether you would like to be considered for the promotion and then have the opportunity to stay in the program an additional year. If you chose to go for the promotion, the leadership team would decide between two options: option 1, you get promoted to manager, or option 2, you don't get selected. Well, I didn't get accepted. For a time I wondered if there was something I could have done differently, and honestly, the answer was no. God revealed to me that He had moved on from that place and ultimately allowed me to move on as well. But move on to where? That was a question I wallowed in for seven months—and not by choice. During this time, it felt like no matter how impressive my résumé (which landed me interviews with companies like GE, McKinsey, and Amazon) was, I couldn't land a job! The feedback I kept getting was, "You don't seem to want this job." Needless to say, I had a lot of time to reflect and be with God, which I took advantage of. Each day I would wake up and spend four to five hours praising God, acknowledging His goodness and love for me. He gave me clarity and understanding, and in this most uncertain time of my life, I felt the most connected, secure, and blessed I had ever felt. Although I technically didn't have a job, God still provided me with my same salary for seven months. I never missed a paycheck, and when I landed a job, I had an everlasting peace and connection that only time could have built. The experience taught me discipline, how not to be moved by the situation or circumstance in front of me. I also had peace during the storm, when everyone around me could only see the rain and the wind crashing against my boat. I realized that while I was with God and while God was with me, I had no reason to worry. I trusted Him fully and accepted His Word. His presence was too grand to focus on the problem. I was immersed in His love and grace and felt so incredibly blessed to have the opportunity to get to know Him and reveal pieces of who I am. I led by example. My family and friends were in awe of how comfortable I was in that uncomfortable position. They wondered if I was aware of the severity of the problem. The truth is, I was but didn't care because I knew who was on my side. My being was peaceful, and that peace helped others learn more about Jesus, which put them at peace as well.

Key takeaway:

> The things you have learned and received and heard and seen in me, practice these things, and the God of peace will be with you. But I rejoiced in the Lord greatly, that now, at last you have revived your concern for me; indeed, you were concerned before, but you lacked opportunity. Not that I speak from want, for I have learned to be content in whatever circumstances I am. I know how to get along with humble means, and I also know how to live in prosperity; in any and every circumstance I have learned the secret of being filled and going hungry, both of having abundance and suffering need. I can do all things through Him who strengthens me. (Philippians 4:9–13 NASB)

Stand on His Word.

Think about a time when your situation looked and felt terrible, but the opposite of what you expected happened. What would you say was the root cause of that? How did you involve God in this situation?

Leading with the Opposing Deed

As mentioned earlier in the chapter, the opposite of peace is strife (struggle) and dissensions (disagreements). To break down what this truly means, I would rephrase it to say that the opposite of peace is the struggle to endure, to gain, to resolve, and to struggle for victory. It's a fight, a competition, and a conflict. It's disagreement. It's war. It's you striving to make something happen instead of trusting God to make it happen. It's you being ambitious and potentially not aligning your will to the will of God. According to Psalms 37:23 (NASB), "The steps of a man are established by the Lord, and He delights in His way."

Your willingness must shift from your will to God's will. To make that shift, stop thinking about where you're going and start focusing on whom you're going with. It's not about going where you want to go but about going where God sends you. When God sends you, He will sustain you. On the other hand, when you go on your own, you're responsible for sustaining yourself. As I said, I went seven months with no work and got paid. God provided and allowed me to experience the exact opposite of what people usually experience, which is no work, no pay. It was a season when I walked with the Lord and waited for Him to show me what He wanted me to do, giving Him time to develop my character and set the pace for my next step. And *then* I got a call. Someone was offering me the position! Praise God! May His will be done.

Not long after I started that job, I began to recognize that I didn't have much time to do anything else. Those early morning praise breaks were cut short because I worked with a team in India and had a standing 7:00 a.m. call that I was expected to lead. That meant in my mind that I needed to wake up at 5:00 a.m. to prepare by doing the work instead of spending time with God. This was day in, day out. I was working late nights and weekends to make sure I got up to speed quickly to start delivering results. I hated the feeling of being "new" and the idea of not knowing something, so I put in extra hours to learn. I was tired, sleepy, frustrated, not eating correctly, and neglecting all the relationships I cared about having. Although the people at work were happy and saw my "value," all I could think was, *How am I going to continue this way?* Within my first three weeks on the job, I was nominated for and received an Above and Beyond award. It was this award that brought me back to my senses. Very upset at myself for getting it, I realized that it was all me doing the work and that I had not involved God in any of it. It was at that moment I recognized I wouldn't be able to sustain this level of performance without God. I started striving for something God had already given me.

Here I was sabotaging myself and my relationships for what, the fear of uncertainty? I believe God gave me this job to show me how quickly I could revert to old habits and forget what He had already done. During my slow season, I grew the most—so much so that I thought, *Cool. Thank You,*

God, I can take it from here. This is where I started outpacing God's grace (divine enablement) to do what God had planned for me to do, instead of me doing what I thought God would have wanted for me. This revelation allowed me to slow down and remember where I needed to be. It allowed me to get back in the presence of God and ask Him what I should do and focus on next. When I got back in His presence, accepted His Word (Psalms 37:23), and learned from this situation, I had peace and clarity with regard to my next step.

The reality is, it's easy to get ahead of ourselves. When you find yourself not making time for God, know this as an indicator that you may be outpacing His grace. Also, recognize that the Lord said there will be tribulations but to be of good cheer as He has already conquered the world.

Realization: There will be tribulations, *but* … That *but* is essential. It is used to introduce the exception. The exception is that the Lord has already conquered it. Be of good cheer because although you face it, you don't have to follow it. Follow the Lord, and then that problem becomes your platform for the glory of God.

Chapter Summary—Peace in Essence

God made a covenant with us, a promise of safety, blessings, and prosperity. Understand this is an *always* kind of promise that's never void. Although things happen that look dangerous, cursed, or poor, don't allow your fear of getting hurt, being forgotten, missing out, or running out distract you from receiving the promise of God. Remember, He promised you will live in safety and that no one will make you afraid. To access your peace, you must remember His promise and what He said in Philippians 4:6–7: Don't worry about anything; instead, pray about everything. If you have enough faith to believe, that's all you have to do. To keep the peace, we must trust God and fix our thoughts on the Lord. To activate peace, we need Jesus as He is our peace. Without Him, internal peace isn't available for us. It is Jesus's actions that allow us to have a relationship with God. His doings made peace between God and us. Without Jesus, we can't access the Father, meaning we're cut off, which also means we're disjointed from the promises of God as well. To know the promises requires us to know Jesus, and to know Jesus, we must have the faith to believe He is Lord and died for us so that we may live. To have peace, we must invite Jesus into the situation that is causing us struggle or disagreement. Jesus instructs us to come to Him, accept His teachings, and learn from Him.

As a leader and believer, you have to know there is a reason for the struggle or disagreement. The task isn't to understand the logic but to recognize that the reason was a decision. And sometimes you experience conflict even when it wasn't your decision that caused it to happen. Either way, don't focus on the reason or whose fault it is; focus on Jesus and what God said. Because although God didn't cause it, He'll use it.

Steps Forward

Think about how to apply what you've learned. Outlined below are tactical steps for you to take so as to allow the Holy Spirit to work and produce peace in your life:

- **Identify** what situation(s) is causing you to struggle or generate conflict.
- **Identify** the decision that caused the situation to happen. Write it down.
- **Think** about God's promise and remember a time you felt peace. What made you receive that peace?
- **Assess** what your thoughts are fixed on. Is that thinking blocking you from what God said? If yes, pray for God to help you realign your thoughts in a way that allows His Word to be on your mind.
- **Identify** a scripture (choose one from the chapter or one that comes to mind through your study) that reminds you of the peace God gives and how God's Holy Spirit produces peace in your life.
- **Repeat** the scripture until it resonates and you have memorized it.
- **Quote** the scripture every time you're struggling and thinking you can't overcome the problem.

- **Write** what you are giving more thought to than you're giving to God and what you can do to realign those thoughts so they become fixed on God.
- **Pray** over what you wrote.
- **Thank God** for providing you with clarity and understanding about how to realign your thoughts and receive perfect peace for all things you go through.

End-of-Chapter Activity

Use this time to self-reflect and understand how this information is relevant to your life. Spend time with God now to worship Him and invite Him in as you complete the following questions:

1. How are you finding peace in the work you're currently doing?
2. If you currently don't have any peace, what's the problem or concern creating the struggle or conflict?
3. What can you do specifically to get in the presence of God and learn from His teachings?
4. What tactical step are you willing to commit to taking so as to shift your eagerness to do something while you wait on God's provision to do what you're supposed to do right now?
5. What makes committing to taking this one step important for you?

Closing Scripture

"Do not be anxious about anything, but in every situation, by prayer and petition, with thanksgiving, present your requests to God. And the peace of God, which surpasses all understanding, will guard your hearts and your minds in Christ Jesus" (Philippians 4:6–7 CSB).

SECTION II
HUMANWARD RELATIONSHIP

Dear brothers and sisters, when troubles of any kind come your way, consider it an opportunity for great joy. For you know that when your faith is tested, your endurance has a chance to grow. So let it grow, for when your endurance is fully developed, you will be perfect and complete, needing nothing.
—James 1:2–4 (NLT)

CHAPTER 4

THE FRUIT OF PATIENCE

God blesses those who patiently endure testing and temptation. Afterward they will receive the crown of life that God has promised to those who love Him.
—James 1:12 (NLT)

Chapter Introduction

In section 1, we discovered the fruit of the Spirit that allows us to develop a relationship with God that overflows to those around us. To love, be joyful, and have peace, we learned it's a posture, our positioning our thoughts and attention toward God. In this section, we will learn how to develop a relationship with others, which first requires us to have patience.

When it comes to leadership development, we all recognize and value the growth opportunity. We understand the importance of being seen by others as a mature, experienced leader. Whether we're starting out or have been in a particular domain for a while, we seek learning opportunities to say we're focusing on our development. We can find ways to speed up the process by going through course work or a rigorous leadership development program. But no matter how much we read or how much we experience, one thing is sure: we have to go through something to get developed. "Going through" is the key because it isn't always easy. Going through it is what it sounds like—hard work. Often we see the development and want it. We get excited about how the growth will change us for the better and bless both us and our family in numerous ways, but we forget to see the construction.

Think about building a house. You work with the architect or contractor to design it. After you see a prototype of the finished project and approve the development, you trust the contractor to oversee the job and to be held responsible for completing the vision and staying on budget. The contractor then hires subcontractors to do the work. According to an article I read, "How House Construction Works" by Marshall Brian, the first step is site preparation.

Site preparation: During this phase, a bulldozer is required. The main goal of this step is to clear the things that are in the way of building the foundation. Depending on the site, it's not enough to just clear away the things. One must also pour concrete in the trenches to ensure the foundation is level and stable. Once the concrete is poured, it takes weeks to cure to full strength (or longer depending on the weather). This means that right after the moment the concrete is poured, a necessary step in securing the foundation, nothing will happen while the curing is taking place.

Next, the framing crew comes in to build the floor to set the house on. Then they assemble the walls up from the floor. It is important to note that these walls are interrupted with windows and doors that require a header (beam) to give the wall enough strength over the window or door to support the roof. The exterior walls go up by being nailed to bind the corners. Once the exterior walls are up, the interior walls are put in. Now it's time for the roof. Once the roof is secured, it's time to enclose the windows and doors. The windows and doors must be shipped, so this process is pending the time of arrival. Once you have the windows and doors installed, it's time to dress the house with brick or siding; do the plumbing, electrical work, insulation, and drywall; install heating and air conditioning, cabinets, and counters; hook up the house to the water and sewage; and provide wall trim, paint, carpet and/or tile. Then comes the punch list. Right when you think you're done and it's time to move in, the contractor inspects the house and tabulates all the problems. The contractor then assigns the appropriate subcontractors to come back to fix all of these. Only at this point are you able to move in.

I simply described the build of a basic house to illustrate that you can't have the house without the construction. When you first find out you have the resources to build a home, you see it as a blessing. You recognize what it would mean for you and your family, and you thank God for it. But then comes the work, a process you have to go through to develop that house.

The critical difference between a blessing and a curse is the time you wait. The most essential takeaway from this example is site preparation. This is the step that builds your foundation. What your house will be able to endure depends on how the foundation is built. In Matthew 7:24–27 (NIV), Jesus says,

> Therefore everyone who hears these words of mine and puts them into practice is like a wise man who built his house on the rock. The rain came down, the streams rose, and the winds blew and beat against that house, yet it did not fall, because it had its foundation on the rock. But everyone who hears these words of mine and does not put them into practice is like a foolish man who built his house on sand. The rain came down, the streams rose, and the winds blew and beat against that house, and it fell with a great crash.

Key takeaway: Patience allows you to build endurance. It is the inspection, the testing of your faith, that produces endurance. So if you want to develop your character and grow in different areas of your life, then you must learn to wait well.

What is patience? Patience is waiting with calm or calmly waiting. It's as Billy Graham put it: "the work of God when one endures difficult situations and people without losing one's composure." Patience is a virtue that requires the Holy Spirit to produce this fruit in our lives. To fully understand patience as a concept, you must understand God's promises. It's much more difficult to wait on something you're not sure is yours.

However, when you know that what is meant for you will be available for you, you won't have to worry about getting it. Rick Warren puts it this way: "Waiting patiently on God is a statement of faith and humility." It's you trusting and being dependent on God to endure the process without worry. It's standing on God's Word as your foundation, remembering scriptures like Hebrews 6:10–15 (NIV):

> God is not unjust; He will not forget your work and the love you have shown Him. ... Show this same diligence to the very end, so that what you hope for may be fully realized. ... Through faith and patience inherit what has been promised ... When God made His promise, He swore "I will surely bless you." ... And so after waiting patiently, [you will] receive what was promised.

There will be times you feel like giving up, but remember, don't trust your feelings. Trust God.

Key takeaway: We read in 1 Peter 5:6–7 (MSG), "So be content with who you are, and don't put on airs. God's strong hand is on you; He'll promote you at the right time. Live carefree before God; He is most careful with you."

You know you have patience when you are content with your situation, when you trust God's timing, and when you know that when the time is right, you will receive the promise. It's when you realize you're not waiting on God; He's waiting on you to develop your faith and build your character. You must be able to recognize that delay is not denial and not be quick to get stressed out over what doesn't appear to be going your way. You must not get frustrated with the process, or jealous of others' progress, because endurance is being aware that these are "punch list" symptoms, an indicator you're in the final phase of receiving the blessing.

Leading with Patience—Jesus in Action

According to 1 Corinthians 10:13 (NLT), the Bible says, "The temptations in your life are no different from what others experience. And God is faithful. He will not allow the temptation to be more than you can stand. When you are tempted, He will show you a way out so that you can endure." Understand you are not exempted from temptation. We all will be tempted just as Jesus was. When we are tempted, we must recognize it for what it's worth: an opportunity to defeat the devil by not giving in to the temptation. Jesus demonstrates what to do when we're tempted in Luke 4:1–13. There is an order as to how the devil approaches you, and it is important to know he will give all he has to convince you to choose the temptation instead of God's Word and God's way out. That said, you will always have a choice, a choice between good and evil, right and wrong, love and lust, etc. To understand how Jesus was tempted and how it applies to our lives, let's break the scripture into sections.

Section 1: Being Spirit-Led and Tempted

The leading: Luke 4:1–2 (NIV) states, "Jesus, full of the Holy Spirit, left the Jordan and was led by the Spirit into the wilderness, where for forty days he was tempted by the devil. He ate nothing during those days, and at the end of them, he was hungry."

- **Point #1.** Being full of the Holy Spirit does not exempt you from being tempted.
- **Point #2.** Sometimes the Spirit will take you into the wilderness to allow you to choose between defeat and development.
- **Point #3.** The wilderness is a training camp for you to defeat the devil and become more like Christ. It's an honor to be led by the Spirit into the wilderness as (1) you know the Lord is with you and that He will help you find a way out and (2) it's a sign He trusts that you can overcome the temptation and choose what is right. Remember what was said in 1 Corinthians 10:13: "He will not allow the temptation to be more than you can stand." He sent you to reveal the truth.

The temptation: Luke 4:3–4 (NIV) reads, "The devil said to him, 'If you are the Son of God, tell this stone to become bread.' Jesus answered, 'It is written: "Man shall not live on bread alone."'"

- **Point #1.** The devil knew where Jesus was and how He was feeling (hungry), so he used His hunger (a desire from within) to tempt Him. Notice that it was the most prominent and immediate need at the time.
- **Point #2.** Jesus addressed what the devil said with God's Word: "It is written …" Notice how it wasn't a present or future state answer; it was past tense with the sense that God has already addressed this and hence Jesus only needed to reiterate what He said.

Section 2: Enduring

The temptation: We read in Luke 4:5–8 (NIV), "The devil led him up to a high place and showed him in an instant all the kingdoms of the world. And he said to him, 'I will give you all their authority and splendor; it has been given to me, and I can give it to anyone I want to. If you worship me, it will all be yours.' Jesus answered, 'It is written: "Worship the Lord your God and serve Him only."'"

- **Point #1.** The devil, not God, leads you into temptation. The Lord does not attempt to give you anything, because He has already given you everything.
- **Point #2.** The devil tries to deceive you into serving him, providing you with an if-then statement, whereas the Lord says in John 12:26 (NIV), "Whoever serves me must follow me; and where I am, my servant also will be."
- **Point #3.** Jesus addressed the devil's attempt with God's Word.

The temptation: Luke 4:9–12 reads, "The devil led him to Jerusalem and had him stand on the highest point of the temple. 'If you are the Son of God,' he said, 'throw yourself down from here. For it is written: "He will command his angels concerning you to guard you carefully; they will lift you up in their hands so that you will not strike your foot against a stone."' Jesus answered, 'It is said: "Do not put the Lord your God to the test."'"

- **Point #1.** The devil will tempt you into doubting who God has called you to be and then try using your exact words against you

in effort to confuse you into believing what he is saying, to create doubt in what you know to be true.
- **Point #2.** The devil starts catering his attempts to mimic what you say to convince you it's you who's really saying or thinking whatever thought he was trying to tempt you with.
- **Point #3.** Jesus addressed the devil's attempt by reframing "It is written" as "It is said," acknowledging that He didn't get fooled by the devil's sophisticated effort and yet again answering with God's Word.

Section 3: Overcoming Temptation

The devil gives up. Luke 4:13 states, "When the devil had finished all this tempting, he left him until an opportune time."

- **Point #1.** You have more endurance than the devil as the Holy Spirit gives you the power to endure the temptation. When the devil recognizes you have the endurance to withstand his temptation, he leaves you alone as he knows he will be defeated. However, understand that you will be tempted again.
- **Point #2.** The devil recognizes that the only chance he has at destroying you is to wait until it is inconvenient for you or to catch you feeling vulnerable. Note that this is the most opportune time for the devil to trick you into disobeying God's Word.
- **Point #3.** When you feel like your thought is going against what you know to be true, what God specifically said, or causing an objection, it's the devil's opportune time.

Understand you will be tested. However, know that for every test, there is an option to pass or fail. With the Holy Spirit, you can never fail. As noted in the Lord's Prayer, "Lead us not unto temptation but deliver us from evil." The Lord will never lead you into temptation, and He will always deliver you from evil. The request, make it your prayer. Acknowledge that you need God involved to travel alongside you to ensure you have the strength and ability to withstand. Trust Him, and know that if He leads you into the wilderness, it's for growth padded with grace as your divine enablement to pass the test.

Key takeaway: When your faith is tested and when you are tempted, you have an opportunity to develop.

To better understand the test, think about the exams you've had to take that allow you three attempts to pass with a 70 percent or higher. In this scenario, you log into the exam and attempt to take the exam off the knowledge you already have, and maybe you just get a preview of the questions on the exam. Let's say when you finish the exam, your score is revealed, and you get 65 percent. You go back through to review the questions you got wrong, and you think, *Okay. Process of elimination. It's not that, so maybe it's this.* You decide to go back and retake the exam, and this time you get a 68 percent. You panic because now you only have one more chance to get this right. Instead of using the process of elimination, you look at the items you got wrong and open the textbook to refamiliarize yourself with the text. You study the chapters that address the things you got wrong. You go back to the test and take the exam. On this attempt, you pass. You're not concerned with whether it was a 70 percent or 100 percent; you just need to know you passed. Recognize that the test and results are given by God, whereas the attempt is allowed through the devil. That said, it's important that you know that the devil can only attempt. He can't get you to "log in" to take the test, he can't get you to endure the test, he can't get you to eliminate the things that don't work, and he can't get you to open the text and study God's Word to pass the test. He doesn't have the final say on whether you pass or fail the test.

We sometimes think the devil has more control than he does. We believe his attempts will take us out by force, by attacking our life, when the truth is, his attempts are meant to be an act of *trying*. To try often means to make an unsuccessful effort (an attempt).

So, instead of trying, you trust. God doesn't want us to try anything, because He knows the plans for our life, plans to prosper us and not harm us; plans to give us a hope and a future (Jerimiah 29:11). To trust, we must know God's Word, what He's said about our life and current situation, what He's promised us. When you feel tempted, understand it is an attempt. An attempt is an unsuccessful effort unless you try doing the thing you're tempted to do. In that case, it becomes a temptation or a strong enticement to stray from your actual course. The real choice and test of your faith is not whether you give in to the temptation or do the right thing over the wrong thing, but whether or not you're willing either to *try* to do it yourself or *trust* God to do it for you. The choice is between trying and trusting. It's having a constant posture of not trying and just trusting God will do what He said He'd do in His perfect timing.

When your faith is tested, you are tempted. When you are tempted, your endurance (ability to withstand hardship or adversity) has a chance to grow. The temptation is the opportunity you have to make a choice on whether you want to try it yourself or trust God to do it for you. The temptation, seen as a weapon trying to destroy you, is more than that; it's a tool God will use to develop you. No weapon formed against you shall prosper. Notice the scripture says "against you," not "in you." The only way the devil will succeed is if you fall on the sword or, said differently, stab yourself with the weapon only intended to come against you.

Guiding Principles:

1. It's a test with only two options (pass or fail). God is the answer, and He never fails.
2. Remember God's Word: "Be still and know" (Psalms 46:10 NIV) and "Wait patiently for Him" (Psalms 37:7 NIV).
3. Don't try, just trust. The test of faith is whether you try doing it yourself or trust God to do it for you.
4. Only when you fall on the sword will it prosper, not when you come up against it.

As leaders, we sometimes say things like "taking one for the team," and at such times, all we see is the blame someone must claim. As leaders, we feel it is our responsibility to take the blame. However, we must spend a little more time assessing whether the thing we're taking on is a sacrifice or suicide. One requires you to surrender while the other forces you to fall on the sword. Both result in the feeling of destruction and loss. However, one is an offering with an expected promise in return (a lesson learned), while the other is your attempt to solve a problem that was never intended for you to solve.

Here's how to tell the difference:

Sacrifice: You give up.
Suicide: You give in.

I realize earlier in the text, I encouraged you not to give up, to stay the course, and trust God. And that remains true because the Word says, "So let us not get tired of doing what is good. At just the right time, we will reap a harvest of blessing if we don't give up" (Galatians 6:9 NLT). The key here is "doing what is *good*."

To take the blame, you must give up your pride and sacrifice your reputation. You decide to take on the responsibility of enduring the circumstances. You're innocent and don't claim the mistake to be your fault, but your willingness to give yourself up on behalf of your team to save them is purposeful. As stated in Hebrews 12:2 (NLT), "We do this by keeping our eyes on Jesus, the champion who initiates and perfects our faith. Because of the joy awaiting Him, He endured the cross, disregarding its shame. Now He is seated in the place of honor beside God's throne." The act of knowing it's not your fault but enduring it anyway develops you as a leader. It helps you to stay focused on God, to humble yourself, and to grow your character. However, when you fall on the sword (i.e., commit suicide), you take yourself out. You decide it's not worth the fight, and you give in to the idea that it's your fault and your problem and that you deserve to lose.

Simply put, you fail, and you know this to be true because you feel like a failure. In these cases, take a step back and remember that failure is not a person; it is an event. And when you fail, know it is an opportunity to build your faith and trust God because He is the answer. He never fails. Focus on God; trust His Word. When the opportunity presents itself again for you to take one for the team, patiently wait on the Lord to understand the approach. The outcome may feel the same, but the stance is very different.

Personal Reflection

I had just landed the job, and instantly I realized that the job was not what I wanted; however, I recognized that God blessed me with it. It was the job that came after my seven-month waiting period, and while starting the role, I just felt like no matter how I thought about it, it was something God wanted me to do. That said, I convinced myself to give it my all—and that I did. After only three months, I felt burnt out. I was succeeding, and all those around me were ecstatic with my performance. However, I knew it wasn't sustainable. I eventually realized that I was outpacing God, that I was performing the job my way and not consulting with God, hence the reason I felt so exhausted and "in over my head." I took a step back and started to focus on how to invite God in, and shortly after, I was asked to go work with our project team in India for a month. During this time, a recruiter had reached out to me to inform me of a job opportunity. I was not looking, and since it felt so out of the blue, I decided to entertain the idea. *Maybe God wants me to do this,* I thought. I didn't overthink it while going through the job interviews. I simply felt that if it was for me and meant to be, it'd be. At the time my trip to India had been approved, I had made it through the first three rounds of interviews with the hiring manager. The people at the company told me they would try expediting the interview process as they knew I was heading to India for a month. Now a bit concerned, I headed to India wondering what my husband and I should do if I got the job offer. I prayed long and hard and spent time with God, and in my first week of being in India, I got the inclination to move. Week two in India, I received the call that I had gotten the job and that the expectation was that I would start as soon as possible. Well, that made things a bit difficult because I didn't want to leave my current team hanging, not to mention I wasn't in my home country. I asked if I could push the start date out and they said no, but I felt the job was very much in alignment with what God wanted me to do, so I said yes to the offer. That yes meant I had no time to say my farewells, pack, and move to a city that neither my husband nor I had ever considered. It was a shock to our souls and a significant life-changing decision. As soon as I came back from India, I had only two weeks before my start date. This meant I had to submit my resignation to my current company as soon as I landed. That was a bit painful for me because it was a company I had grown up with, that I had given so much to and who had given me so much. However, I felt it was time to move. This move was me trusting God. My husband wasn't entirely convinced that we were supposed to move so quickly or even to the new company and location. Still, he believed that if I felt so aligned with doing it, it must be in God's will for us. So, begrudgingly, we moved.

In our new city, we tried hard in the first few months to like the town, but it just didn't feel like "home." It felt like a stopping place but not permanent. When family and friends asked, "How do you all like it?" we would respond with, "We won't be here long. We're moving to Texas." While patiently waiting, anticipating twenty-four months before we could move to Texas with eight months on the new job, I received a call that my job had been eliminated. This was now the third time that I had abruptly lost my job, so that part didn't concern me. As the conversation continued, my manager followed up with, "You have an option." If I wanted to stay with the company, I would be offered a more significant role, which was my current role multiplied by two, working in Texas. So here my husband and I had thought it would take twenty-four months to transition to Texas, whereas God did it in eight months.

What this situation taught me was two things: (1) trust God, and (2) patiently wait on God.

I recognize that sometimes it's difficult to trust what God is doing because it doesn't seem to make sense. What I have learned is that, that's the thing that makes sense. When what you are going through is beyond your understanding and doesn't seem to follow logic, it's God. So go with it; trust Him. I also recognize that His timing is perfect, and when it's the right time, He will promote you. No need to compare yourself to others and go through the motions of wishing that what is happening for them would happen for you. You don't know what they patiently waited for to get what you're now seeing. Realize it is a process—a process that takes time—and without time you won't be prepared to endure what you're wishing for. I heard that for anything that is given in the wrong season or at the wrong time is a curse, but at the right time, it's a blessing. Rick Warren said in one of his messages, "God tests us with stress before He trusts us with success." Remember that in order to be tested, you have to be in the wilderness, and in the wilderness, you will be tempted to examine your heart. In Deuteronomy 8:2 (NIV), we read, "Remember how the Lord your God led you all the way in the wilderness these forty years, to humble and test you to know what was in your heart, whether or not you would keep His commands." It is essential to know that when you pass the test, God will promote you and deliver you into the promise.

Key takeaway: It takes time, so wait.

To wait calmly is the definition of patience, so when you get caught up in the waiting room, remind yourself not to fear that what you're waiting for will come to pass. Don't worry about how it will come to pass, don't forget God's promises that state He will provide, and don't give up on account of a lack of faith in what God has said.

Leading with the Opposing Deed

On the surface, the opposite deed of patience is impatience. While that is true to some extent, impatience is not a deed that is outlined in the scripture. We're warned not to be impatient and to be of good cheer when it comes to waiting. This makes me wonder why the most logical opposite of patience doesn't seem to fit when describing patience. Well, to be patient or impatient is an "either you are or you're not" sort of thing. There's no choice as to whether you will be impatient; it's just a fact that you are. So I dug a bit deeper to understand the emotions we have while being impatient, especially when it comes to business. What I gathered was that jealousy and envy, two deeds of the flesh listed in the scripture (Galatians 5:19–21), are the opposite of patience. It's your becoming moved by your situation that makes it a deed of the flesh.

Let's break this down using Mark 5:21–43, the story of Jesus raising a dead girl and healing a sick woman. To set the stage, Jesus, on a boat, was drawing near to a crowd. He got out of the boat, and Jarius, a synagogue leader, fell at His feet, pleading that Jesus come with Him to lay hands on His dying daughter. Jesus agreed. As He and Jarius walked through the crowd, a woman touched the hem of Jesus's garment. Jesus stopped and turned to the crowd, asking them who touched Him. His disciples thought it was a ridiculous question seeing that there were so many people around and pressing in on Him. Everyone was touching Him. However, Jesus knew power had left Him, so He stopped to see the person who had received the power. A woman came forth and told Jesus her story that she had an issue of blood that the doctors couldn't heal. She said that she thought if only she could touch Jesus, she would be healed. Jesus then told her that her faith had healed her and to go in peace. While this was happening, Jarius was waiting for Jesus to come with Him to save His daughter.

While waiting for this woman to receive her miracle, Jarius got word that his daughter had died. Jesus overheard Jarius's messenger tell him, "Don't bother the teacher. She's dead," and Jesus said, "Don't be afraid; just believe." At this time, Jesus took His closest disciples (Peter, James, and John) and went with Jarius to his home to see his daughter. When they arrived, Jesus noticed a lot of commotion and said, "Why all this commotion and wailing? The child is not dead but asleep." Jesus took the parents and three disciples into the room where the daughter was lying and said, "Talitha koum!" (Little girl, I say to you, get up!) Verse 42 says, "Immediately the girl stood up and began to walk around (she was twelve years old)."

What's interesting is that when we read this story, we see faithfulness. We understand that in both Jarius's case and the case of the woman with blood, faith is what allowed the miracle to happen. However, there is an underlying story here for us to catch, and that is about the delay. If you, for a moment, think about the woman with the issue of blood, you find out in the scripture that she had this issue for twelve years. When you think about Jarius, he had a twelve-year-old dying as he was waiting on Jesus to come with him to save her. On the surface, Jesus was on His way to save the little girl, but the woman with the issue of blood stopped Him in His tracks and got healed. Think about the level of patience Jarius had to have to wait on Jesus to save a woman in the crowd while fearing his little girl would die. The very thing he was witnessing was the very thing he was hoping for. Jesus stopped en route to saving Jarius's daughter in order to save a woman who had simply stopped Him along the way, only for Jarius to get word while waiting that his daughter had died. Can you imagine how Jarius must have felt? I would imagine he was stressed, frustrated, and jealous, prepared to have a pity party for himself while being envious of this woman because it appeared she had received the blessing meant for his daughter. Jesus recognized that Jarius was validated in feeling that way and reassured him not to be afraid and just believe. At that point, Jarius had a choice to either focus on what had just happened or patiently wait, believing Jesus for the miracle. Jarius chose not to give up and took Jesus to the girl anyhow. And upon His Word, immediately she got up.

What Should You Take Away?

What feels like a distraction, the things that make you stop and/or that delay you from moving forward, is a faith-building stop. You're going in the direction of your destiny, and everything along the path crowding you, pressing in on you, making you at times feel like it's slowing you down is for miracles and healing. That crowd needs you. They're part of your journey because once you get to your destination, it's you bearing and them supporting. You're already on a mission, heading where you need to go. The things pressing in on you have been assigned to you because you are capable of being the solution to those matters. When something or someone touches you in such a way, you have to turn around and understand who or what touched you, know it was a faith stop to make you/them/it well. With regard to whatever is being delayed as a result of this stop, remember that God said, "Don't be afraid; just believe." The thing that is delayed is waiting for you to arrive, and when you get there, it'll immediately get up.

What's interesting is the title of this story, "Jesus raises a dead girl and heals a sick woman," although the sick woman appeared to get healed first. The moment Jesus got off the boat and Jarius fell at His feet, the girl was saved. The crowd or the delays along the way couldn't have affected Jarius's miracle because it was already done. However, the way he waited on Jesus determined how quickly Jesus got to where Jarius wanted Him to be. The sick woman appeared to get her miracle before Jarius. Still, the reality is that Jarius didn't realize that this woman had been ill for twelve years, since the time the little girl was born. For her, this miracle wasn't an overnight success, although those around witnessing what had happened may have thought it was. They didn't see the pain she had been through. The crowd watching probably thought it was unfair that she had gotten healed when Jarius had gotten to Jesus before she did. Others may have even blamed Jesus for stopping and not getting to the situation on time. The crowd may have felt that the woman was selfish, seeing that Jesus was on His way to do something, but she stopped Him in His tracks to heal her first. What seems to be the right order may not always appear to happen in order. Before you grow jealous or envious of someone else's blessing, remember that you've already received yours. It's less about obtaining the blessing and more about waiting for it. When you feel like there is a delay, realize that the purpose of delay is to build your character and faith. Don't fear, worry, forget, or give up on what God has already raised you from. Trust His Word, and know that it's not about the wait but about how you wait that determines when you receive what God has already given you. Your posture of patiently waiting on God is a statement of your faith, standing still while witnessing someone else's blessing. This lets God know that you're humble and not willing to move forward without Him, that you are depending on Him and choosing only to move when He does. It's the knowledge that what is for you will be for you no matter how long it takes for you to get it.

Realization: God doesn't hurry; He's not trying to get somewhere on time. His timing may not feel convenient, but it is perfect. He will never come early or get there late; He will always be there in time. God's timing is always right, and He can do anything immediately. So although you feel like time is slipping away, know that our time is not God's time. A delay does not mean denial; it's merely an opportunity for us to develop our character and faith. We're not waiting on God; He's waiting on us.

Chapter Summary—Patience in Essence

God's timing is the timing for us, not the arbitrary deadlines we set for ourselves. How do we know when we should accomplish something or succeed? We must take a step back to ask: Who told us that was the time frame? How did we pick that timetable to do or have a particular thing? What has convinced us that in five years we're going to be in a specific place doing a particular thing? It's nice to have goals and aspirations, and actually God wants us to. He has placed desires in our hearts so that we may know His will and know what we are supposed to do. However, just because we have a desire to do or have something does not mean we also control how and when we get it or do it. That's God's role. When we know who, we don't need to know how, because our responsibility in this arrangement is simple: to seek the kingdom of God. In Matthew 6:33 (NASB) we read, "But seek first His kingdom and His righteousness, and all these things will be added to you," and Psalms 37:4 (NASB) states, "Delight yourself in the Lord; and He will give you the desires of your heart." The key is being in God's presence to involve Him and invite Him in. Ecclesiastes 3:1 (NASB) states, "There is an appointed time for everything. And there is a time for every event under heaven." That said, it's not worth it to us to duplicate work in trying to figure out when God is going to appoint us and guide us (in everything).

To fulfill the desires of our heart, ultimately we need Jesus to ensure it is the right time (a blessing) and not a curse. The key is to wait patiently on God's timing. Think of God's role as being like a global positioning system (GPS). Think about when you're driving and you're unaware where you're going. The directions are programmed in the GPS, and no one else is in the car to help you look ahead at the steps, so you have to trust that the GPS is doing what it is supposed to do. You're driving for a while, and the GPS isn't saying anything. You wonder if you're still going the right way, but you're hearing nothing, so you look at the GPS to see if there is any indicator you're going in the wrong direction. Then the GPS says, "In a quarter mile, turn right." As you approach the turn, the GPS says, "In five hundred feet, turn right." Nervous and in fear that you won't arrive at your destination on time, you do indeed get there. The GPS isn't continually talking. It directs you when directions change. In a similar way, continue doing what you're doing until God tells you to do something different. He will always inform you when something is coming up or when it's time to do something different. You just have to be patient and calm enough to hear His direction. If the radio is too loud or you're distracted in any way, you may miss what He says. Still, the beauty of God is that He's patient with us all and will reroute your path to get you to your intended destination. Move when God tells you to move, and when He doesn't, be still. Psalms 37:7–9 (ESV) reads, "Be still before the Lord and wait patiently for him; fret not yourself over the one who prospers in his way, over the man who carries out evil devices! Refrain from anger, and forsake wrath! Fret not yourself; it tends only to evil. For the evildoers shall be cut off, but those who wait for the Lord shall inherit the land." Remember, the reason we have to wait is that it's not yet time, and in due time, God's timing shall come to pass. When we know this, our wait will be a lot more carefree because we know that God has appointed the time and that in His time, what comes upon us will be a blessing. Know that the blessing will always be preceded with a test to ensure we're ready. Upon passing, we'll receive the blessing. Enter the wilderness knowing that the Holy Spirit is with you, giving you the power to overcome and step into what God has for you.

Steps Forward

Think about how to apply what you've learned. Outlined below are tactical steps for you to take so as to allow the Holy Spirit to work and produce patience in your life:

- **Identify** what situation(s) you feel are delayed or moving slower than you would have hoped.
- **Identify** what about the situation requires your patience. Write it down.
- **Think** about God's timing, and remember a situation when He came through for you "just in time." What happened at the moment you received your blessing? What did you do that unleashed it?

- **Assess** how you wait on God, knowing what you know now about waiting. Is there anything blocking you from receiving God's blessing? If yes, pray for God to help you realign your thoughts in a way that allows you to endure the test.
- **Identify** a scripture (choose one from the chapter or one that comes to mind through your study) that reminds you of Jesus's patience and how His Holy Spirit produces patience in your life.
- **Repeat** the scripture until it resonates and you have memorized it.
- **Quote** the scripture every time you're struggling and thinking you can't overcome the situation.
- **Write** what about the situation is making you stressed, frustrated, or jealous and what you can do to cease your attempts to falling on your sword and instead remember God's Word and make the sacrifice.
- **Pray** over what you wrote.
- **Thank God** for providing you with clarity and understanding about how to realign your effort to glorify God and receive patience for all things you go through.

End-of-Chapter Activity

Use this time to self-reflect and understand how this information is relevant to your life. Spend time with God now to worship Him and invite Him in while you complete the following questions:

1. How are you choosing to patiently wait on God in the work you're currently doing?
2. If you currently don't have patience, what is the problem or concern creating your inability to be patient?
3. What can you do specifically to get in the presence of God, read His Word, and learn from His teachings?
4. What one tactical step are you willing to commit to taking in shifting your eagerness to waiting on God to give you the provision to do the thing you're supposed to do right now?
5. What makes committing to taking this one step essential for you?

Closing Scripture

"For what credit is there if, when you sin and are harshly treated, you endure it with patience? But if when you do what is right and suffer for it you patiently endure it, this finds favor with God" (1 Peter 2:20 NASB).

CHAPTER 5

THE FRUIT OF KINDNESS

*Be kind to one another, tenderhearted, forgiving
one another, as God in Christ forgave you.*
—*Ephesians 4:32 (ESV)*

Chapter Introduction

Around Christmastime, most individuals, whether they believe in Jesus or not, experience holiday cheer and may even participate in extending acts of kindness to strangers. The most common act of kindness I've seen is paying for the bill of the customer behind you. The idea is to make their day and hope they pay it forward. It's fun to see how long it lasts and to be able to share how someone made your day today, so you made someone else's day. It's beautiful to pay it forward and even more beautiful when you're the recipient of the payment. So if it feels so good, why don't we do this sort of thing more often? Why is it we wait for a particular season to show acts of kindness? I think it's because it's hard to do, so we have to find a reason (e.g., it's Christmas). It's difficult to show kindness to those who aren't showing kindness to us. It's challenging to be a leader in a dog-eat-dog world where kindness is seen as a weakness and to act kind anyhow.

Interestingly, the only time most people are willing to be kind is when it's accepted and when someone else is kind to them first. Well, it's easy to show kindness to those who show kindness to you, but Luke 6:36 (NIV) says, "But love your enemies, do good to them, and lend to them without expecting to get anything back. Then your reward will be great, and you will be children of the Most High because He is kind to the ungrateful and wicked." The question becomes how you will show that same act of kindness to those you feel don't deserve it, to those who act hateful toward you and despise your being. How do you be the bigger person to show kindness to those who are ungrateful and do more evil than good? You first recognize that to be kind when the other person has done nothing to deserve your kindness is by the power of the Holy Spirit. It is the Holy Spirit that produces this type of behavior in you, making the requirement that you invite God into your interactions so that you have enough compassion and forgiveness in your heart to treat the other person you're interacting with, with kindness. Kindness is more than just a simple act of niceness; it is a disposition of grace. To define what kindness is, we must first understand what grace is.

Grace, according to the *Merriam-Webster Dictionary*, is unmerited divine assistance. Breaking down the word *unmerited*, we discover that it means "not adequately earned or deserved." In essence, it's favor, showing mercy to others and forgiving them whether they deserve it or not.

What Is Kindness?

Kindness is a disposition of unearned and undeserved assistance provided to others by the grace and mercy of God given unto you. You can only extend favor when you receive favor. This requires you to know where your favor comes from. If you look to the world to give you favor, that is considered unjust, not fair. However, the favor of God is just that: not fair. It's given to you in the form of blessings, although you've done nothing to receive them (undeserved). Since you've done nothing to receive them, it's seen as a gift (unearned), a present you didn't have to work for, a present you didn't have to pay for, a present given to you simply to enjoy. When you recognize that you have favor and God has shown you kindness, what's stopping you from paying it forward?

To be kind, you need to remember that it's not actually about what the person has done or is doing to deserve your favor. It's about recognizing when God showed you favor and, as a representative of His kingdom, you

THE FRUIT OF KINDNESS

sowed that same kindness unto others. In Romans 2:4 (NIV) we read, "Or do you show contempt for the riches of His kindness, forbearance, and patience, not realizing that God's kindness is intended to lead you to repentance?" Notice it is a question. Kindness is about awareness, realizing it is not a position of absent respect but a position of forgiveness.

God's kindness is displayed in Nehemiah 9:16–17, 19 (NIV):

> But they, our ancestors, became arrogant and stiff-necked, and they did not obey your commands. They refused to listen and failed to remember the miracles you performed among them. They became stiff-necked and, in their rebellion, appointed a leader in order to return to their slavery. But you are a forgiving God, gracious and compassionate, slow to anger and abounding in love. Therefore, you did not desert them. ... Because of your great compassion, you did not abandon them in the wilderness. By day the pillar of cloud did not fail to guide them on their path, nor the pillar of fire by night to shine on the way they were to take.

Even when we deserve to be punished, let go, and forgotten, God still provides. He is gracious and compassionate, He is slow to anger, and He will not abandon us in the wilderness. That is kindness, the kindness that God wants us to display as His children. It is not our job to punish or judge others. It is our responsibility to love them, show compassion, and not be quick to anger when they do something not to our liking.

How do you know whether you're being kind? Remember what it means to love one another: to have joy by focusing on God and not your situation; to display peace even when things get rocky because you know your house is built on solid rock; and to have patience by recognizing the situation as an opportunity for you to develop your faith and character. The reality is that you need all the other fruit described (love, joy, peace, and patience) to be kind to others, showing them favor, compassion, and mercy. The moment you are provoked and feel as though you're about to judge another person's situation and character, remember the miracles God has performed for you, the mercy He's given you, the compassion He's shown you, and the grace He's extended to you. Don't be quick to judge or think the person doesn't deserve it, because the truth is, neither do you.

Leading with Kindness—Jesus in Action

Jesus was passing through Jericho when Zacchaeus, a wealthy tax collector, was eager to see who Jesus was. While standing in the crowd, Zacchaeus realized he wouldn't be able to see Jesus, so he climbed a sycamore tree to get a good view of Him while He was passing by. Picking up the story in Luke 19:5–7 (NASB), the Bible says, "When Jesus came to the place, He looked up and said to him, 'Zacchaeus, hurry and come down, for today I must stay at your house.' And he hurried and came down and received Him gladly. When they saw it, they all began to grumble, saying, 'He has gone to be the guest of a man who is a sinner.'" The moment you read this verse, you are under the impression that Jesus knew Zacchaeus. However, earlier in the scripture, the Bible says that Zacchaeus was trying to see who Jesus was. Jesus looked at him and called him by name. For context, tax collectors were seen as sinners. They were rich from getting over on people, charging them more than they should have for taxes. People of that time despised tax collectors and considered them undeserving of Jesus's attention and love. So with Jesus's passing by and recognizing and appearing to know the tax collector, you can only imagine how the people witnessing this judged Him. Then Jesus went on to say He was staying at Zacchaeus's house. The people couldn't understand. In their minds, Jesus had violated norms by dining with and associating Himself with sinners.

What's interesting about this story is that Zacchaeus started to apologize to Jesus about his wrong doings, mentioning how he would pay those he had cheated back. However, Jesus was only concerned with welcoming him and making Zacchaeus feel noticed. Jesus didn't start out with "Zacchaeus, you've wronged people." Instead, Jesus led with kindness. He allowed Zacchaeus to approach Him, and He received Him gladly. This interaction was unpopular, and although those watching had a lot to say about how Jesus was interacting with Zacchaeus, Jesus showed kindness anyway. He

THE FRUIT OF KINDNESS

displayed mercy and forgiveness by saying He was staying at his house. Can you imagine the president or CEO of a large company passing by and, seeing a janitor peeking out from the hallway, saying, "John, come over here. I'm staying at your house tonight." How would you react as the leader on the CEO's executive staff who doesn't know or trust the janitor? It's effortless to judge the people in the story judging Jesus, but the reality is that we are like them more often than we'd like to believe.

Key takeaway: No matter which people others think are undeserving of your love and respect, have mercy on them and forgive them for whatever their offense is. Out of love and respect, lead with kindness. In Luke 6:37–38 (NIV), the Word says, "Do not judge, and you will not be judged. Do not condemn, and you will not be condemned. Forgive, and you will be forgiven. Give, and it will be given to you. A good measure, pressed down, shaken together and running over, will be poured into your lap. For with the measure you use, it will be measured to you."

Guiding Principles:

1. **Be visible.** Separate yourself from the crowd, not so that you will be seen but so that you will see Jesus.
2. **Remember, Jesus knows who you are.** Jesus knows your heart and knows you by name. He will always look for you and receive you gladly.
3. **Know that the grumbling of others doesn't matter.** No matter what people grumble about or how true their grumbles may be, your kindness toward them will always overpower your confrontation with them.
4. **Stop yourself from being judgmental.** Don't be quick to judge. Every time you choose not to show mercy or forgive someone for a mistake (big or small), you are a part of the crowd that's witnessing and grumbling. Don't be classified as "they" in the story, but rather be seen as the named person who gladly received the guest.
5. **Lead with kindness.** It's not for you to say whether or not someone deserves kindness or has done enough to earn kindness. That's just

it. You lead with kindness because at some point you've received it when you didn't deserve or earn it.

Key takeaway: It's only challenging to lead with or show kindness when you have formulated a judgment about the person you are meant to be kind to (which is everyone).

That judgment is hindering you from trusting that person enough to show kindness to him or her. Say that you know the person and think of him as being a "prick" or as someone who would take your kindness for weakness; there is a judgment blocking you from being kind. Assess the thoughts you're having about that person to better understand what's hindering you from showing him kindness. Then remember that your kindness is a disposition of grace, which is a gift to the person that is undeserved and unearned, and your giving of it pleases God.

Personal Reflection

I remember like it was yesterday having a friend take me to McDonald's to fill out a job application. I was sitting in the lobby filling out the form, and I remember feeling like, *This job will be fun. I hope I get it.* I turned my application in to the manager on duty, and he said, "Wait here. The store manager is here and can interview you now." In my head, I didn't feel prepared for an on-the-spot interview, but I thought, *Sure. It shouldn't be that bad.*

Meanwhile, my friend was in the car, eating an apple pie and laughing at me. I start talking to the store manager. It went well, and just like that, I got my first job! Fast-forward two weeks: I am unsatisfied. The job wasn't what I expected it to be. I was pulling weeds out of the garden; taking the trash out; cleaning the lobby and bathrooms; sweeping and mopping the floors; refilling sauces, bags, and cups; making coffee; and filling up the ice in the beverage machines. And when it was busy, I would do fries. The icing on the cake? Everyone in management was rude and disrespectful.

I was *over* it, and to be honest, I cried about it a few times. One day the general manager came in while I was mopping and, in passing, said to me, "Oh, you're still here? I thought you would have quit by now." That stopped me in my tracks, and that moment became the moment I kicked off the project Kill Them with Kindness. Literally at that moment, I told myself I was going to be fake by showing up every day with a big smile on my face. Because I realized they were doing all they were doing to me on purpose. They were trying to break me. I was showing them how bothered I was, and they were using that against me. During my next shift, I didn't pout; I smiled and asked questions. I was nice even when they were mean. I greeted customers and did everything the managers had told me to do without complaining. I eventually was put on cashier duty and no longer was asked to sweep or mop the floors. I wasn't assigned to the lobby but was told that if there were no customers, I should wipe down tables in between customers. I had someone available to me to fill up the ice and stock the sauces, bags, and cups. I was then moved to the table where I was running the line. Then I was asked to go to other locations when a fill-in was needed. That same general manager who walked by saying, "Oh, you haven't quit yet," was the same person who asked if I would be open to doing a McDonald's commercial. He said I was such a great representative of how they want all their associates to be, and he wanted me to display that behavior.

This experience taught me more than I ever knew it would. What started as me being fake kind with a phony smile whenever management asked me anything or said or did anything that made me upset, I'd win, in return frustrating the managers. What I found is that eventually they changed! No. The reality is, I changed. Over time I forgot to fake my kindness. I began genuinely smiling and helping managers and showing them how valuable and humble I was in doing all the grunt work with a smile on my face. My kindness wasn't my weakness; it was my strength and my decision. I made up my mind that I wasn't going to let the people or the work get in the way of my smile. Although those managers didn't deserve to be treated with kindness and definitely hadn't earned it, my choosing to be kind anyhow changed my perspective on them and the job. In turn, it also improved their view of what I was capable of doing. It allowed me to enjoy what I was doing and the people I was working with. To quote Zig

Ziglar, "If you go looking for a friend, you're going to find they're scarce. If you go out to be a friend, you'll find them everywhere."

The world's view of kindness often is that you're a pushover, but God's view of it is that you're an overcomer.

Luke 6:35 (NIV) states, "But love your enemies, do good to them, and lend to them without expecting to get anything back. Then your reward will be great, and you will be children of the Most High because he is kind to the ungrateful and wicked."

Recognize that when ungrateful and wicked people are placed in your life, you have the option of seeing them as a test you're choosing to pass or fail. Understand that the answer needed to pass is the act of showing them kindness. And for every test passed, you get promoted, rewarded for your good works.

Leading with the Opposing Deed

As we learned earlier in the chapter, when we're unable to show kindness, it is because we have a judgment blocking our ability to act kind or display grace. To better understand the blockage, we must understand judgment. According to the *Merriam-Webster Dictionary*, judgment is the process of forming an opinion or evaluation by discerning and comparing. Said differently, we sometimes struggle to show someone else kindness because we have developed an opinion about that person. An opinion is a thought that's in our mind, a belief we have that hinders us from being kind to that person. In executive coaching, we call this a limiting belief. Limiting beliefs may have been, at some point, validated or even justified. However, there comes a time when you must forgive and let go, and upon letting go, you show kindness to that person. As we read in Romans 2:1 (NIV), "You, therefore, have no excuse, you who pass judgment on someone else, for at whatever point you judge another, you are condemning yourself, because you who pass judgment do the same things." Your judgment of the other person is an indicator that you feel you are better than she, that you're able to judge because you do no wrong and have never sinned.

The truth is, we are all sinners, and because we are, our kindness shown to those who are wicked is God's way of helping them to remember to turn away from sin. It's not meant for you to feel weak or soft but for you to be strong and a partner in the kingdom to reach other people. Your acts of unexplainable kindness are what counts because that's when you are good when you have every right in the world's eyes not to be. This gives God glory; this kindness makes people question because it is outside the norm. Bystanders become curious and may even ask how you were able to be kind. And when they do, there is only one answer: "By the grace of God."

To think that our kindness is weak is immature. It is through kindness that turns others away from sin. Our kindness is an indicator that we are thinking about someone other than ourselves and something other than how we feel. It's showing compassion for those who make mistakes and being the *one* to show grace and mercy. By not doing this, we are selfish, thinking about ourselves. Our beliefs about the other person are limiting us from being used by God. Romans 2:4–6 (NLT) says, "Don't you see how wonderfully kind, tolerant, and patient God is with you? Does this mean nothing to you? Can't you see that his kindness is intended to turn you from your sin? But because you are stubborn and refuse to turn from your sin, you are storing up terrible punishment for yourself. For a day of anger is coming, when God's righteous judgment will be revealed. He will judge everyone according to what they have done." Your being kind isn't for you, and it requires you to think beyond yourself. As a leader, if you try getting ahead by putting others down, passing judgment on your counterparts or direct staff, you are allowing self-ambition to hinder your growth.

Philippians 2:3–4 (NIV) says, "Do nothing out of selfish ambition or vain conceit. Rather, in humility value others above yourselves, not looking to your own interests but each of you to the interests of the others." When you live this scripture, you have a disposition of grace. You show kindness to all those you encounter. So the moment you strive to get ahead or formulate bitterness toward another, know that you are leading with the opposing deed of kindness, namely, self-ambition. The Bible says in Ephesians 4:31 (NASB), "Let all bitterness and wrath and anger and clamor and slander be put away from you, along with all malice." There's no magic pill, just you letting go.

My mother was an executive assistant for many years at a Fortune 500 company. When I was a young child, she would come home saying to treat everyone, from the janitor to the CEO, the same and know that they all put on pants just like you do. As a child, I didn't fully understand what she meant—not until I started in Corporate America and the dog-eat-dog world I was in. That one nugget allowed me to show the same level of respect for everyone. It allowed me to shine light in situations where there was none, and it left a standing opinion in my mind, namely that titles mean nothing. Treat everyone with kindness and do good no matter who is watching.

Chapter Summary

Kindness is a disposition of grace, an undeserved and unearned gift you give for one reason: because it has been given to you. We always look for an in-the-moment reason why we should or shouldn't be kind to someone, when the reality is that we already have a reason: Jesus. Jesus has shown and continues to show us kindness. Instead of looking for our kindness in the world, we need to look to Jesus, who always receives us gladly without judgment. Our coworkers, family, and friends may not deserve our kindness, but they do deserve compassion, a mild temperament, and forgiveness. It is not our job to judge them for who they are and what they've done but rather to be representatives of God, displaying the grace He has given us. As a leader, you must remember the rule of reciprocity. If you judge, you will be judged; if you condemn, you will be condemned; and if you forgive, you will be forgiven. However, how you treat your direct reports and those around you will be paid forward. So if you want to be treated and approached with kindness, you must handle and approach others with kindness. It's not your job to judge. It's your job to hold your team accountable and to discipline as needed to ensure results. However, to formulate an opinion that keeps you from being unbiased is immature and is a sign that you must invite God into your leadership.

Steps Forward

Think about how to apply what you've learned. Outlined below are tactical steps for you to take so as to allow the Holy Spirit to work and produce kindness in your life:

- **Identify** a situation that makes you feel judgmental and ambitious.
- **Identify** what about the situation makes you ambitious. Write it down.
- **Think** about a time when you put someone else's interests above your own at work. What was the outcome of your doing something that didn't seem to be in your best interests? How did you feel after you had done it?
- **Assess** how often you lead with kindness. Knowing what you know now about kindness, is there anything blocking you from being kind to others? If yes, pray for God to help you realign your thoughts in such a way that allows you to forgive and let go.
- **Identify** a scripture (choose one from the chapter or one that comes to mind through your study) that reminds you of Jesus's kindness and how His Holy Spirit produces kindness in your life.
- **Repeat** the scripture until it resonates and you have memorized it.
- **Quote** the scripture every time you're struggling and thinking you can't overcome the situation.
- **Write** what about the situation is making you bitter, judgmental, and unwilling to be kind, and then write what you can do to examine your belief and what needs to happen to change your opinion.
- **Pray** over what you wrote.
- **Thank God** for providing you with clarity and understanding about how to realign your belief so as to glorify God and receive His grace to display for others.

End-of-Chapter Activity

Use this time to self-reflect and understand how this information is relevant to your life. Spend time with God now to worship Him and invite Him in while you answer the following questions:

1. How are you choosing to lead with kindness in the work you're currently doing?
2. If you currently struggle with showing kindness, what opinion have you formed that's keeping you from being kind? Of the things you can control, what needs to happen for you to let the matter go?
3. What can you do to get in the presence of God, read His Word, and learn from His teachings?
4. What one tactical step are you willing to commit to taking to shift your judgment in such a way that allows you to act kindly toward everyone?
5. What makes committing to taking this one step essential for you?

Closing Scripture

But when the kindness and love of God our Savior appeared, he saved us, not because of righteous things we had done, but because of his mercy. He saved us through the washing of rebirth and renewal by the Holy Spirit, whom he poured out on us generously through Jesus Christ our Savior, so that, having been justified by his grace, we might become heirs having the hope of eternal life. This is a trustworthy saying. And I want you to stress these things, so that those who have trusted in God may be careful to devote themselves to doing what is good. These things are excellent and profitable for everyone. (Titus 3:4–8 NIV)

CHAPTER 6

THE FRUIT OF GOODNESS

For we are God's handiwork, created in Christ Jesus to do good works, which God prepared in advance for us to do.
—*Ephesians 2:10 (NIV)*

Chapter Introduction

Leadership is a service, and those looking to you for leadership are your customers. As with any service provider, your most important success metric is your service level, which is how your customers rate the service you provide. Your rating should always be described as good. Not great, not excellent, not amazing, not extraordinary, but good. Good represents the fruit of the Spirit and signifies that you are helpful and a blessing, and that you serve. We as a society have made being good mediocre. We think that being good isn't enough, so we say things like "Why be good when you can be great?" Then when great gets played out, we want to be excellent. When excellent become underrated, we become amazing, and when amazing isn't big enough, we become extraordinary. My point is that being great, excellent, amazing, or extraordinary is an exaggeration of being good. The truth is, we're not capable of always being good. Ecclesiastes 7:20 (NLT) says, "Not a single person on earth is always good and never sins." We strive to be better than good, but we fail to recognize our limitations as humans. We were born with sin, as stated in Romans 3:23 (ESV), "[we] all have sinned and fall short of the glory of God." That said, only God can truly be great, excellent, amazing, and extraordinary.

The best we can do is serve as an image of God, which by the Holy Spirit allows us to be a reflection of God's goodness because God is good. In Genesis 1:27, 31 (ESV), we read, "So God created man in His own image, in the image of God He created him; male and female He created them. … And God saw everything that He had made, and behold, it was very good."

God created us in His image, and of all His creation, it was only mankind who He said was very good. God is pleased with us because He knows our potential. He created us in His image, which allows us to display goodness in His likeness. So at best we can be very good, which the world would describe as great, excellent, amazing, or extraordinary. That said, when you receive such a compliment, treat it as a sign that you are working in excellence through the power of the Holy Spirit to be good at what you're doing. Titus 3:8 (ESV) says, "The saying is trustworthy, and I want you to insist on these things, so that those who have believed in God may be careful to devote themselves to good works. These things are excellent and profitable for people." It is your belief in God and your devotion to His works that He has already prepared for you that makes you good, which means you are excellent and profitable to others.

In 2 Timothy 1:9 (NLT), we read, "For God saved us and called us to live a holy life. He did this, not because we deserved it, but because that was His plan from before the beginning of time—to show us His grace through Christ Jesus." No matter how much you've done to get where you are, remember that you're not there because of what you or someone else has done. You're there because it was God's purpose for your life. So the moment you are described as great, excellent, amazing, or extraordinary, understand those are God's qualities, and the credit for your coming across that way belongs to God. The description is an indication that you are imitating the Lord. For you were created in His image. First Peter 2:9 (NLT) says, "For you are a chosen people, a royal priest, a holy nation, God's very own possession. As a result, you can show others the goodness of God, for He called you out of the darkness into His wonderful light." Realize that it is not by your ability but by God's. When you are complimented on your work because it is excellent and profitable to others, the praise belongs to God. As you are using His qualities to do the work, making you a representative of God, fulfilling His purpose and His calling on your life.

What Is Goodness?

Goodness is the excellent qualities of God.

Goodness is our ability to serve others, to provide excellent "customer" service by the power of the Holy Spirit, producing the skills required to serve according to God's plan. Goodness is what attracts people to the God inside us, which means we must trust the Lord in all we do. Psalms 37:3 (NLT) says, "Trust in the Lord and do good, then you will live safely in the land and prosper." So if you trust in the Lord and do good, you will live safe and prosper. Doing good is so essential that your safety and prosperity depend on it. The good news is that all you have to do is first trust God and second do good by showing others the goodness (excellent qualities) of God.

Often when people are studying the fruit of the Spirit, kindness, and goodness are talked about together with kindness representing the disposition and with goodness being the description of how you act as a person. In essence, it is thought that the two mean the same thing, but presented differently to the world, one is internal (kindness) and the other external (goodness). This is the reason for the two being outlined as two separate fruit. I agree this is true, but I feel there is more to goodness. To go a little further, let's talk about goodness with a view toward purpose. Ephesians 2:10 (NLT) says, "For we are God's masterpiece. He has created us anew in Christ Jesus, so we can do the good things he planned for us long ago." This verse indicates that goodness isn't just a description of kindness. It is an expectation. The reason God created and saved us was so that we may serve. The Bible says, "It is He who saved us and chose us for His holy work, not because we deserve it but because that was His plan" (2 Timothy 1:9 TLB). We don't deserve to be in the position we're in or to have the level of influence we have, but we have it because God chose us to do His works. He trusts us to serve and be good at doing that.

He has given us the resources to perform His holy work and has shown us great mercy. Because of this, we are to dedicate ourselves to His service.

Goodness is validation that Jesus is in our life. We were born sinners, which represents all our human weaknesses that Jesus came to die for so we may be reborn. Goodness is a reminder that we were born in this world but are not of this world. To illustrate this, let's look at what happened. God created mankind on the sixth day and said His creation was very good. After that, the serpent (Satan) came and tempted Eve, and as a result of Adam and Eve's disobedience, sin (human weakness) entered the world. Spiritually, the number six symbolizes mankind and human weakness, the evils of Satan, and the manifestation of sin. Then Jesus came and died for us so that we may be saved and become heirs of the kingdom. Jesus walked the earth and displayed how we should act through the fruit of the Spirit: in love, joy, peace, patience, kindness, goodness, faithfulness, gentleness, and self-control. Here goodness is positioned as the sixth fruit. Goodness is more than just a description of kindness. It is a reminder that our weaknesses and sins are battles already won by Jesus. Through His Holy Spirit, we can produce goodness in our lives so that we may serve others and show them the goodness of God through our good deeds.

Leading with Goodness—Jesus in Action

Proverbs 16:3 (NASB) reads, "Commit your works to the Lord, and your plans will be established." When we think about goodness, it is essential to associate it with our works. Goodness has to be shown, and as defined in this chapter, that means showing the excellent qualities of God. Your works should display your character and allow others to see that you are a good person. In Luke 6:45 (NASB), we read, "The good man out of the good treasure of his heart brings forth what is good, and the evil man out of the evil treasure brings forth what is evil; for his mouth speaks from that which fills his heart." What you produce is directly correlated to who you are as a person, and the good news is that it's all behavioral, and behavior can be learned and changed. You are not a good person because you're merely good. Only God is good. You were born into sin but also in the image of God. We are each like a picture, the visual image of God that can be

The Fruit of Goodness

impactful in all different shapes and sizes, whether abstract or figuratively. With an image, you can look at it and see how well the moment was captured and take notice of the details in the picture to determine that it is good. You can have a feeling or emotion toward what has been captured. You can see how excellent the quality of the picture is and determine if the image is clear. If it has a high definition or high resolution, you may even say things like, "That is a good picture" (or an excellent picture, or an amazing picture, or an extraordinary picture). However, the picture itself isn't those things; the moment that was captured was. As we think about how we go about doing our work, we must understand how we're capturing the moments. Recognizing that there are so many ways to go about doing that well, the Bible says in Proverbs 16:9, 20 (NASB), "The mind of man plans his way, but the Lord directs his steps. ... He who gives attention to the word will find good, and blessed is he who trusts in the Lord." Seeing how it is your mind that plans out your way, it is critical to ensure your mind is renewed in Christ, which is done by staying in His Word, abiding in Him, and trusting Him to lead the way.

In Mark 10:17–27 (NASB), we get Jesus's perspective on being good and how to display goodness. The Bible says, "As He was setting out on a journey, a man ran up to Him and knelt before Him, and asked Him, 'Good Teacher, what shall I do to inherit eternal life?' And Jesus said to him, 'Why do you call Me good? No one is good except God alone. You know the commandments, "Do not murder, Do not commit adultery, Do not steal, Do not bear false witness, Do not defraud, Honor your father and mother."' And he said to Him, 'Teacher, I have kept all these things from my youth up.'" Notice that when the man approached Jesus, he didn't just call Him a teacher; he also described Him as "good." However, Jesus made mention of what the man had called Him and answered with "No one is good except God alone." Then He responded to the man by saying he should follow the commandments to inherit eternal life. The Bible goes on to say in verses 21–22, "Looking at him, Jesus felt a love for him and said to him, 'One thing you lack: go and sell all you possess and give to the poor, and you will have treasure in heaven; and come, follow Me.' But at these words, he was saddened, and he went away grieving, for he was one who owned much property." Jesus could have just answered the man's question of "What shall I do to inherit eternal life?" with "Follow the commandments." However, Jesus wanted to help the man and teach His disciples by examining the man's heart, telling him what he was missing and what he could do not only to inherit the kingdom but also to have treasure in heaven.

What is interesting about this text is that Jesus doesn't allow the man to describe Him as good and corrects him in calling Him good. Then He shows God's goodness by revealing to the man out of love the thing he's lacking. Jesus showed compassion to this man even though He knew what the man was going to choose. Out of the goodness of His heart, Jesus informed him. It's as if Jesus did not want to set false expectations for the man, allowing him to walk away thinking all that was required of him was to follow the commandments. Jesus also shared with him how his treasures on earth translated to his riches in heaven. Jesus revealed to the man his heart and allowed him to choose. Jesus also used this situation as a teachable moment by saying, "It is easier for a camel to go through the eye of a needle than for a rich man to enter the kingdom of God." The scripture goes on to say, "They were even more astonished and said to Him, 'Then who can be saved?' Looking at them [His disciples], Jesus said, 'With people, it is impossible, but not with God; for all things are possible with God.'" In this verse, God reveals the importance of Jesus as our Savior. Without God the Son (Jesus), we can't enter the kingdom of God. We are not able to save ourselves by choosing that which we can touch, see, and hear. We are able to be saved by following Jesus and trusting that the good treasures of our heart will bring forth what is good and that those treasures will be available to us in heaven.

Guiding Principles:

1. **Only God is good.** To be described as good is a reflection of what you've done and have produced. Every time you are described as good or with a derivative of the word *good*, it's a moment to glorify God for His goodness because it is the display of God in you that makes you good. Remember, *good* is the adjective being used to describe or clarify the noun (person, place, or thing).

2. **Goodness or the lack thereof is tied to your inheritance.** Doing what is right only gives you access to heaven. However, the work you do is contingent on what's in your heart. We read in Matthew 6:21 (NASB), "For where your treasure is, there your heart will be also." And as stated in Luke 6:45 (NASB), "The good man out of the good treasure of his heart brings forth what is good; and the evil man out of the evil treasure brings forth what is evil; for his mouth speaks from that which fills his heart." What you have here on earth is not a direct correlation to what you will have in heaven. The Bible warns us in Matthew 6:19–20 (NASB), "Do not store up for yourselves treasures on earth, where moth and rust destroy, and where thieves break in and steal. But store up for yourselves treasures in heaven, where neither moth nor rust destroys, and where thieves do not break in or steal." Check your heart and understand where the glory is being placed. Is it being placed on work or on God?
3. **Your good works are an indicator of your wealth in heaven.** It is important to remember that God wants to bless you and provide you with wealth here on earth. However, it is a result of your good works. Experiencing blessings on earth means you've displayed the goodness of God, that you have given Him the glory for what was or is being accomplished. You are acknowledging that only God is good, so for you to produce what is good, you recognize it is God in you that reflects what is good, which can only be good when you feel love toward the works. Love is the currency in heaven.

Key takeaway: A formula to remember is this: Knowing Only God Is Good + Doing What's Right + Following Jesus = Eternal Life with Treasures.

The more you love, the more currency you have to do amazing things and display the goodness of God.

Personal Reflection

Fruit is identified by what you display. It is the way you act. Matthew 7:17–18 states, "So every good tree bears good fruit, but the bad tree bears bad fruit. A good tree cannot produce bad fruit, nor can a bad tree produce good fruit." In this scripture, you are considered the tree. It is crucial to understand how a tree becomes a tree. The gardener plants the seed then waters it so that the seed can grow. Once the seed starts to sprout and take root, it begins to grow upward. After years of nurturing, the tree starts bearing fruit. A good root can only produce good fruit, which means a bad root can only produce bad fruit. So the question becomes, how do you know if you're producing good or bad fruit?

Think about what people are getting from you. If they were to spend a week in your presence, what would they take away? How would they feel—happy, sad, good, bad? Our fruit is what others eat; it's the nourishment we provide to others. As the saying goes, "You are what you eat." So if the fruit is the way you act, it can be consumed by those who are around you. They become what you feed them. As a leader, you need to know that those looking up to you are eating your fruit. They are digesting it and becoming what they eat. Look at those you oversee and ask yourself how long will they be able to survive by eating the fruit you are producing.

"You are what you eat" became true for me when I realized I was a leader. For so long we go around thinking that what we do doesn't matter and that how we act affects only us. But the reality is that how we act affects everyone connected to us. It is also possible not to produce anything and become the person standing around eating off everyone else's plate. I remember sitting in a vacant conference room telling my coach about the process of waiting to hear if I was getting promoted. There were nine or so spots and forty people who were being considered. My roommate and I were both being considered. We were working on the same extended team, sitting in what we called the "bullpen" with about fifteen others. Everyone knew we would find out in April whether we were promoted to manager. So right around the end of February, the questions started to come: "How are you feeling?" "Do you think you'll get it?" "What are you doing to make sure you get selected?" Then in March, there was full-blown pressure. Everyone in the bullpen was stressed, full of anticipation to see what the outcome would be. I would walk in the room and feel this sense of anxiousness, which made me feel stressed about receiving the result. I didn't feel worried or concerned, but also I was purposely not thinking about the promotion. In my mind, I had only put my name in the hat to be considered and decided to allow fate to run its course instead of having to decide for myself. I genuinely felt that if the job was meant for me, it'd be for me, and if it wasn't, then it was because God had something else for me to do. I didn't try sharing that perspective with my team, so I wasn't giving them anything other than the fact that I was unbothered. In the midst of this, however, I started to feel stress and anxiety, but I was not entirely sure why. I thought, *I'm unbothered and will continue doing my job as if I'm not up for promotion.* I was just being myself and working how I normally worked.

I shared this with my coach, and she started to explain to me how energy works. As she described the principles, I quickly began to see that I was taking in my coworkers' energy. They were concerned and worried for me, stressing out about what would happen to me. Without my giving them anything to go off of, their energy was starting to fill the bullpen with overwhelm. I and everyone in that room were beginning to consume the energy. Not realizing I was seen as a leader, I quickly realized that I had stopped feeding them; it was becoming a severe case of malnourishment. Again, not realizing how much influence I had, I just decided to send out an email implementing a weekly day of no complaining.

I outlined the ground rules and showed up to the office happy, with positive energy, and held everyone to the ground rules. I wrote a blog to help the team self-assess their energy, did a one-hour-long webinar about happiness, and had everyone take a happiness quiz. To my surprise, people were forwarding my "no complaints day" ground rules, sharing their happiness quiz results, and reaching out to me for ideas to improve their score. The energy shifted very quickly and then multiplied from a room of twenty people to an organization of five hundred people. I started to receive comments like, "I think this blog is amazing—very thoughtful and creative! I found myself reading through and conducting my own self-interview, which had me reflecting on the positive things that I wish we did more of [ultimately the purpose of the blog]. Very creative!" "Love what you are doing. Great topic. ... I am so pumped for the session." "Thanks for an awesome session. Keep it up, and keep it happy."

Now in hindsight, I realize that was fruit. That was evidence of my good works in the period of waiting on the news of whether I got promoted. At that point, it didn't matter because my tree was producing good fruit, which unbeknown to me at the time sprinkled seeds that I am now reaping today.

You are going to bear fruit, and no matter what you want to produce, you are only going to produce what you carry.

So ask yourself, what are you feeding people?

Jesus says in John 15:1–4 (NLT), "I am the true grapevine, and my Father is the gardener. He cuts off every branch of mine that doesn't produce fruit, and he prunes the branches that do bear fruit so they will produce even more. You have already been pruned and purified by the message I have given you. Remain in me, and I will remain in you. For a branch cannot produce fruit if it is severed from the vine, and you cannot be fruitful unless you remain in me."

Every root is either of this world or of God, and only God is good. He is the Source, the Gardener, and Jesus is the Root. You are the branch that is expected to produce the fruit. Where you produce fruit, you are displaying the goodness of God; you are allowing the world to "taste and see that the Lord is good" (Psalms 34:8 NLT).

Leading with the Opposing Deed

We read in Ephesians 5:11 (ESV), "Take no part in the unfruitful works of darkness, but instead expose them." As we look at the foundational scripture of this book, Galatians 5:16–23, we see that it tells us what the works of the flesh are and what the fruit of the Spirit is. There are nine things God considers fruitful work. However, since we are talking about a fruit within that, it is essential to remember what goodness means. It is the excellent qualities of God coupled with our ability to serve others. If we're not serving others, we aren't producing light, and our works become darkness, not serving those around us and hence not fruitful. The Bible warns us in Titus 3:9 (ESV), "Avoid foolish controversies, genealogies, dissensions, and quarrels about the law, for they are unprofitable and worthless." God is not requesting you to make dissensions on His behalf. He is asking you to display the fruit of the Spirit on His behalf because it is produced by Him. To further understand this, let's look at the word *dissension* again. Dissension represents a disagreement that leads to discord. A synonym for *discord* is *dissonance*. When I think about dissonance, I think of cognitive dissonance, which is the condition where a person experiences a contradictory belief arising from some physical trigger that causes them discomfort. Cognitive dissonance is you doing one thing and saying another. It's you knowing what's right but still doing what's wrong. It's knowing the good thing to do but choosing to do the bad. Every time you find yourself in contradiction, take a step back to understand the trigger and root of the decision you're tied to making. What type of fruit will the outcome of your contradiction produce? With what do you need to ask God for help? Is it to align your thoughts with your actions or your actions with your thoughts?

Proverbs 6:16–19 (ESV) states, "There are six things that the Lord hates, seven that are an abomination to Him: haughty eyes, a lying tongue, and hands that shed innocent blood, a heart that devises wicked plans, feet that make haste to run to evil, a false witness who breathes out lies, and one who sows discord among brothers." Your actions matter, in particular what you sow among other people (your fruit). The Bible says the seventh thing is an abomination. The seventh thing listed in the foregoing verse is "one who sows discord among brothers." Interesting enough, all that is recorded are things God hates, but the sowing of discord among others is something He is disgusted and outraged by. God wants us to love others, and our planting disagreements or creating a lack of harmony is the exact opposite of our displaying His goodness. Be mindful of the tension you create, and recognize the conflict your actions create. Your cognitive dissonance impacts how you act, and the way you act is displayed in the fruit you produce. The fruit you produce is an indicator of the seed that is sown, which is a seed that has taken root. You reap what you sow and what was sowed unto you. Understand your power and ability to sow a seed that can take root in others' lives.

Chapter Summary

Goodness is more than a choice to show kindness. It is your ability to serve others and display the highest-quality image of God. It is proof to the world that you love God and follow Him. It is your expression as a person and the opportunity to draw others in to experience the love of God. As leaders, we are people whom others look up to, expecting us to influence their careers and lives positively. They look up to us and feed off our energy, and what we produce they become. In knowing that, you have to remember to inspect your fruit and ensure you are properly nourishing those who encounter you. God doesn't want you to go to work and offend others' religion or convince them to be one thing over another. He simply wants you to serve others and perform deeds that sow seeds that produce good fruit. That is good works, knowing that what you've done, positively affect those you've encountered. Look at your actions and assess what is causing you to act or react this way. For every area of your life, think about whether someone could see that God is the priority of that area, and for the areas you struggle in, invite God in. He can help you uproot the bad seeds sprouting that may have already taken root in your life. He will reveal bad seeds, remove them, and plant new seeds to take root that will allow you to produce good fruit and nourishment to those connected to you. You just have to let Him.

Steps Forward

Think about how to apply what you've learned. Outlined below are tactical steps you may take to allow the Holy Spirit to work and produce goodness in your life:

- **Identify** what energy you give in different areas of your life. Is it positive or negative?
- **Identify** what about your energy is positive or negative. Write it down.
- **Think** about a time when you received a compliment regarding how you made someone feel or a thank-you note for your inspiration. What did the person specifically compliment you

on or say you inspired him or her to do? How did you feel after receiving the compliment?
- **Assess** how often you provide excellent service to others. Knowing what you know now about goodness, is there anything blocking you from being good to others? If yes, pray for God to help you align your thoughts and actions in such a way that allows you to display His excellent qualities.
- **Identify** a scripture (choose one from the chapter or one that comes to mind through your study) that reminds you of the goodness of the Lord and how His Holy Spirit produces goodness in your life.
- **Repeat** the scripture until it resonates and you have memorized it.
- **Quote** the scripture every time your thoughts and actions do not align with producing something good.
- **Write** what about the situation is making you respond or act negatively, what you can do to examine your thoughts, and what needs to happen to change your action.
- **Pray** over what you wrote.
- **Thank God** for providing you with clarity and understanding about how to align your thoughts and actions to glorify God and display His goodness.

End-of-Chapter Activity

Use this time to self-reflect and understand how this information is relevant to your life. Spend time with God now to worship Him and invite Him in while you answer the following questions:

1. How are you choosing to lead with goodness in the work you're currently doing?
2. If you currently struggle with showing goodness, what thoughts have you formed that are keeping you from being good? Of the things you can control, what needs to happen for you to let go the thoughts causing you to struggle?
3. What can you do specifically to get in the presence of God, read His Word, and learn from His teachings?

4. What one tactical step are you willing to commit to taking to improve how you show up and perform?
5. What makes committing to taking this one step essential for you?

Closing Scripture

"Trust in the Lord and do good; Dwell in the land and cultivate faithfulness" (Psalms 37:3 NASB).

SECTION III
INWARD RELATIONSHIP

But when He, the Spirit of truth, comes, He will guide you into all the truth; for He will not speak on His own initiative, but whatever He hears, He will speak; and He will disclose to you what is to come.
—*John 16:13 (NASB)*

CHAPTER 7

THE FRUIT OF FAITHFULNESS

> *For it is by grace you have been saved, through faith—and this is not from yourselves, it is the gift of God—not by works, so that no one can boast.*
> —*Ephesians 2:8–9 (NIV)*

Chapter Introduction

We read in Ephesians 2:7–10 (MSG),

> Now God has us where he wants us, with all the time in this world and the next to shower grace and kindness upon us in Christ Jesus. Saving is all his idea and all his work. All we do is trust him enough to let him do it. It's God's gift from start to finish! We don't play a major role. If we did, we'd probably go around bragging that we'd done the whole thing! No, we neither make nor save ourselves. God does both the making and saving. He creates each of us by Christ Jesus to join him in the work he does, the good work he has gotten ready for us to do, work we had better be doing.

God wants us to understand how the elements of faith, trust, and grace come together through the works of the Holy Spirit. Romans: 12:3 (NLT) states, "For by the grace given me I say to every one of you: Do not think of yourself more highly than you ought, but rather think of yourself with sober judgment, in accordance with the faith God has distributed to each of you." It is common for us to exaggerate what we've done right and to undermine the impact of what we've done wrong.

The three points you should take away are:

1. Grace is a gift.
2. Faith is distributed.
3. Trust is what you do.

To help you further understand your role as a leader and what it means to be Spirit-led, I will break down each of the foregoing points so that you may see that it all lies in your faithfulness in God and the good work He has already prepared for you.

Grace Is a Gift

When you think about what a gift is, you think of a present, something given by someone else that you can utilize in some kind of way. Maybe you can wear it, or spend it, or eat it, or cook it. Whatever was given to you, you must accept or receive it in order to utilize it. Grace is a gift from God, and as with any gift, you must accept or receive it to use it. When we think about what grace is, we see that it is unmerited, undeserved, and unearned. It's free, and what it does is give you divine enablement to do the good work God has already prepared for you to do. As stated in the scripture, "God has us where He wants us … to shower grace and kindness upon us in Christ Jesus." This lets us know that the grace and kindness of God rest in Jesus, and if that is what God wants to give us, we must realize that it is in Jesus. Jesus is our grace, and His Holy Spirit lives in us. If we have the faith to believe Jesus is Lord, who died on a cross to save us, who defeated death (resurrected) and now resides in us, then we can receive Him as our Lord and Savior and hence have access to God's grace in Him. In life, we have received many different gifts, some of which we appreciate and others we wish we could give back. However, it is up to each individual to perceive the value of his or her gift and determine how much or little he or she will utilize it. In Romans 12:6–8 (NLT), the Bible goes on to say, "We have different gifts, according to the grace given to each of us. If your gift is prophesying, then prophesy in accordance with your faith; if it is serving, then serve; if it is teaching, then teach; if it is to encourage, then give encouragement; if it is giving, then give generously; if it is to lead, do it diligently; if it is to show mercy, do it cheerfully."

God may give one person the grace to talk to people and another the grace to think clearly or design a room. He may also give a person the grace to do multiple things—but know it is faith in your abilities to do those things that actually allow you to do them. So not only is faith the requirement to receive grace, but also it is the requirement to perform your good works. We have all fallen victim to feeling we're not enough or that we do not have the right skill to do our job. We also tend to devalue our gift by comparing what we have the grace to do to the gifts of the people around us, thinking, *Little ole me? All I can do is give insight and facilitate the meeting. But So-and-So does a phenomenal job of taking charge and driving results.* You think that giving insight and facilitating a meeting is easy because you've been given the grace to do it.

In contrast, someone else may feel, *If only I can get them all in the room, provide the right insight, and facilitate them in a way to get them all on the same page, I can take charge and drive results.* The truth is that no matter how minor you think your gift is, it is needed. Romans 12:4–5 (NLT) says, "Just as our bodies have many parts and each part has a special function, so it is with Christ's body. We are many parts of one body, and we all belong to each other." Undermining your "little" gift is impacting the greater good. Your "little" gift is the exact thing needed to do big things in the world.

In order to value your spiritual gifts, it is vital for you to have faith, and to have it, you must know how it is distributed.

Faith Is Distributed

For starters, what is faith? According to Hebrews 11:1 (KJV), "Faith is the substance of things hoped for, the evidence of things not seen." Faith is the belief of the things you once hoped for. It's what you believed (past tense), not what you are believing, for. Faith is knowing you already have the thing that hasn't shown up yet. Faith doesn't just show up; you must pursue and grow your faith, which the Bible tells us about in Romans 10:17 (ESV): "Faith comes from hearing, and hearing through the word of Christ." This means that in order to have faith, you must know God's Word, and to get more faith, you must know more of God's Word. Said differently, your faith is measured by how much of God's Word you know and have internalized to the point that you walk it out. The scripture says "hearing and hearing," which indicates it's not a onetime read or listen-to. You must get to the point where you are no longer believing in God's Word but have believed God's Word and know that it is true. So that you know that you know God's Word is true and that the promises of God are yours, you must activate the faith you have. To do that requires you to act. James 2:26 (ESV) says, "For as the body apart from the spirit is dead, so also faith apart from works is dead." Faith without works is dead, so it is essential for us as leaders to recognize that the work we do reflects what we have faith in. The principle of faith applies to everything, not only God. You have to ask yourself what you are hearing and seeing that is convincing your spirit that it's true or that someone is trustworthy. What you give your time to, you will reap the fruit of. Look at the results and responses you're getting and ask yourself, "What have I heard and believed that has allowed me to get this outcome?"

Faith is so simple that it's difficult and potentially a bit tricky to understand. We tend to see faith as only a spiritual word. However, the reality is that faith is the strong beliefs that you've internalized, some of which encourage you to do things better or differently and some that limit you and stunt your growth. The point is, take a closer look at what you have believed in and understand how it has shown up in your life. What actions have you taken to bring those beliefs to fruition? Have these beliefs negatively or positively impacted your daily work? Are you getting the outcome you want? If not, what do you need to start hearing to reverse-engineer what you've believed? For the thing(s) you believe, recognize that it is active, and you can change the present. Assess what you currently believe in and determine if you want to internalize it and have it show up in your life. If you don't, then what do you need to immerse yourself in to change your narrative? Is your work starting to reflect what you believe in? Is it worth continuing? If not, do you know what else is possible for you that would be valuable to you? For the things you are believing for, understand you are in pursuit, so look at what you'll get in return for believing.

For whatever you're experiencing, analyze the outcome and contemplate if it is the outcome you want. If it is, then continue doing what you're doing, because the truth of the matter is, you're doing something to allow it to show up in your life. But if you are not satisfied with the outcome, design the outcome you want and work backward to understand what you need to hear and keep hearing to get that particular outcome. To be a Spirit-led leader, you must stay in the Word to know what Jesus has told us. It will cause you to know that there is no situation, absolutely none, you can go through that hasn't already been addressed in the Bible. Staying in the Word will help you believe that your work becomes a reflection of the Holy Spirit, guiding the good work God has already prepared for you.

Trust Is What You Do

Proverbs 3:5–6 (NIV) says, "Trust in the Lord with all your heart and lean not on your own understanding; in all your ways submit to Him, and He will make your paths straight." To fully understand this scripture, we must understand what trust means. One definition I read says that trust is a firm belief in the reliability, truth, ability, or strength of someone or something. Synonyms for the word are *confidence* and *faith*. To trust is to have faith, and to have faith is to trust. Think about the people and processes you trust. Also think about the ones you don't. Ask yourself how confident are you that these people and/or processes are reliable and will deliver the result(s) you want. For those people or processes you don't trust, what has caused you not to trust? Did they underperform or let you down in any way? Did the process not work? Do you have enough information, or do you need more information, to make an informed decision?

Key takeaway: That which you trust is what you have faith in.

Is what you trust the thing or person you would like to have faith in?

To trust in the Lord, you must have faith in the Lord, and to have faith in the Lord, you must meditate on His Word day and night and hear and keep hearing the Word of God to know that you know you've got it. When you have it, you're open to listening and allowing God to take the lead. God tells us not to lean on our own understanding, making mention of the idea that if we trust Him, we won't have to take the lead; He will. If we submit to Him in how we work and we walk in what we think is the way, He will make our path straight. Well, if it is necessary to know that God will make our path straight, that would indicate that our path wasn't straight before we submitted our ways to Him. We don't know what we don't know, and we have blind spots, but God knows the plans. In Jeremiah 29:11 (NIV), He says, "For I know the plans I have for you, plans to prosper you and not to harm you, plans to give you hope and a future." If you knew that and trusted that, your faith would produce hope and a future—and trust in the Lord.

Now that you understand all three elements, let's discuss how they come together to produce faithfulness.

They come together through the work of the Holy Spirit. The Holy Spirit is often glossed over, summed up as being God's Spirit within us and sometimes considered "woo-woo" if you use the name Holy Ghost. The Holy Spirit is God's Spirit that resides in us because of the sacrifice of Jesus. It's His Spirit that His death and resurrection allowed for us to have access to. Faith is required to trust that Jesus died and rose from the dead to give us hope and a future so that we may live life more abundantly as a result of His living inside us. His Holy Spirit speaks to and guides our spirit. It responds and intervenes on our behalf and removes the weight of the world from our shoulders.

The key, however, is to invite the Holy Spirit in, to decide on whether you want the Holy Spirit to guide and control your day or yourself (flesh) to control the day. In the book *The Holy Spirit*, Billy Graham writes, "When we are yielded with God, we are filled with the Holy Spirit. The Holy Spirit controls and dominates us. Now we are to act on that truth and walk or live with full assurance that God has already filled us, and we are under His control. ... It is by faith I know I am filled with the Holy Spirit. If you are filled with the Holy Spirit, you will produce the fruit of the Spirit." It is essential to understand that *yielded* means to surrender. When we surrender ourselves to God is when we are filled with His Holy Spirit.

The act of surrendering is the act of being dead to sin and alive to God. In Romans 6:11–14 (NIV), we read, "In the same way, count yourselves dead to sin but alive to God in Christ Jesus. Therefore do not let sin reign in your mortal body so that you obey its evil desires. Do not offer any part of yourself to sin as an instrument of wickedness, but rather offer yourselves to God as those who have been brought from death to life; and offer every part of yourself to him as an instrument of righteousness. For sin shall no longer be your master because you are not under the law, but under grace." Remember, we are not exempted from sin, and even being filled with the Holy Spirit, we fall short of the glory of God. We are not without fault, so it is critical to get present with God each day and pray that He shows us our sin so that we may repent and submit and walk in obedience to Him. Also, this scripture tells us that we are no longer a master to sin because of grace. However, that is not an indicator for us to go out and sin because we are saved by grace. We read the following in Romans 6:15–18 (NIV):

> What then? Shall we sin because we are not under the law but under grace? By no means! Don't you know that when you offer yourselves to someone as obedient slaves, you are slaves of the one you obey—whether you are slaves to sin, which leads to death, or to obedience, which leads to righteousness? But thanks be to God that, though you used to be slaves to sin, you have come to obey from your heart the pattern of teaching that has now claimed your allegiance. You have been set free from sin and have become slaves to righteousness.

Each day we must choose to empty ourselves and surrender to God in order to be filled by the Holy Spirit, which means that being filled with the Holy Spirit is a daily activity. Billy Graham reminds us that the filling of the Spirit is not feeling; it's faith, trusting God's promises. And by the grace of God, our work can be blameless.

Key takeaway: The Holy Spirit is our guidance and strength, something we must be filled with daily, which requires us to repent and surrender to God. It is by faith that we have believed that the Holy Spirit is guiding us, enabling us, and strengthening us to endure the work. It is by God's grace that our work can be valued as above average, pure, and unblemished. Not because we are pure and unblemished but because God is, who resides in us.

As stated earlier, our work is the outcome of our faith. Grace is what allows our work to be seen as good. The Holy Spirit guides us in performing the good work we do. Your task in all of this is to trust this to be true. When you trust God's Word, you believe in His promises. When you believe His promises, you internalize them, which allows you to build your faith, which comes by hearing and hearing the Word of God. You received grace and surrendered to God in order to be filled with the Holy Spirit. The filling of the Holy Spirit allows Him to take the lead. When He does, it is not by our might or effort that things get done but through the Holy Spirit leading us. The Holy Spirit is pushing, pulling, and carrying us so that we may not get bogged down with the burdens of life. This makes us be able to shine light onto others, reflecting the goodness and kindness of God.

To be faithful is to be full of faith. To have faithfulness is to be fully confident and committed to what we have faith in.

Leading with Faithfulness—Jesus in Action

Mark 11 outlines the story of Jesus cursing a fig tree. It starts off with Him walking up to the tree with the expectation that there would be fruit. However, as He approached, He saw that there was no fruit. The Bible says that it was because it was not the season of figs. However, Jesus says to the tree in Mark 11:14 (NIV), "May no one ever eat fruit from you again," which His disciples hear Him say. The next day the tree had withered from the roots, which shocked the disciples. Peter remembers that it was the tree Jesus had cursed the day before. He said in amazement, "Look," indicating that he was surprised that the tree had died at the very word. Jesus goes on to explain to His disciples the reason for this.

In Mark 11:22–25 (NIV) Jesus says, "Have faith in God, truly I tell you, if anyone says to this mountain, 'Go, throw yourself into the sea,' and does not doubt in their heart but believes that what they say will happen, it will be done for them. Therefore I tell you, whatever you ask for in prayer, believe that you have received it, and it will be yours. And when you stand praying, if you hold anything against anyone, forgive them, so that your Father in heaven may forgive you your sins." Jesus spoke into that fig tree with full expectancy that no one would ever eat fruit from that tree again. He had faith in His Word. Now this may seem like a light story to describe Jesus's faith in action, but the practicality of it is what's important. Your words matter, and when you speak them, they hold power. As a leader, you most likely talk more than others, so you must recognize that speaking the truth and saying what you mean is critical for the growth and success of those you're leading.

Let's break down the story a bit to understand how this applies to your leadership.

Point #1. Jesus had a need: He was hungry.
Point #2. Jesus approached the fig tree with the full expectation there would be fruit.
Point #3. It did not matter that there was a reason for there not being fruit; Jesus cursed the tree for not having fruit.
Point #4. After speaking into the fig tree, He walked away and proceeded to do what He was doing.
Point #5. Those watching were surprised that what He had spoken came true.

When you have a need, approach the solution with the full expectation that it will be fruitful. If it is not but it should be, apply your faith by speaking a word into it, stating whatever you desire to come true. Then walk away and continue doing what you were doing, knowing that what you spoke will go forth. Jesus gave a clear description of how this works. He said, "If anyone says to this mountain, 'Go, throw yourself into the sea,' and does not doubt in their heart but believes that what they say will happen, it will be done for them. Therefore I tell you, whatever you ask for in prayer, believe that you have received it, and it will be yours."

Key takeaway: Anyone can apply faith by following the principle of speaking it, believing it, and expecting it to happen.

Guiding Principles

To be a Spirit-led leader, you must have faith that you are filled with the Holy Spirit and are now under His control. When the Holy Spirit takes over, He is guiding and empowering us. This knowing requires us to walk in the faith that we have been filled with the Holy Spirit and are living in light of this truth. We are to realize that it is a fact that our old nature (our flesh) hasn't physically died. We are encompassing our new identity (the Holy Spirit in us) and deciding to live according to that. If we believe this and know it by faith, and if we are filled with the Holy Spirit, then we will produce the fruit of the Spirit, which others will take notice of. Realize that applying faith and having faithfulness are different in that faith is an action and faithfulness is a belief. To produce faithfulness, you must apply the following principles daily:

1. **Seek to understand God's Word.** Remember, faithfulness is defined as being fully confident and committed to what you have faith in. To grow your faith, you must know God's Word. The Bible tells us faith comes by hearing and hearing the Word of God.
2. **Pray that God reveals your grudges and sins.** In Mark 11:25 (NIV), Jesus says, "And when you stand praying, if you hold anything against anyone, forgive them, so that your Father in heaven may forgive you your sins."
3. **Confess and repent.** Once you know your sins, confess them and ask God for His forgiveness. This is important because it allows you to empty yourself to make room for His Spirit.
4. **Submit to God; be obedient.** Do this by realizing there is a choice you have to make each day, a decision to invite the Holy Spirit into

your day or to go forth to do things by yourself. By submitting to God, you are deciding to trust Him and have faith in His plan. He will allow the Holy Spirit to lead and guide you throughout your day. Be obedient by following the direction of the Holy Spirit.

5. **Have faith.** Have faith that every time you take the foregoing actions, you are filled with and guided by the Holy Spirit, which allows you to produce the fruit of the Spirit.

The fruit of faithfulness is the requirement for all other fruit to be produced. It is the acknowledgment that you need to be filled with the Holy Spirit to be controlled by the Holy Spirit. It is applying your faith, trusting God's Word, and knowing that it is by grace you are even eligible to do the good work God has already prepared for you to do.

Personal Reflection

For most of my life, I've been close to God. However, there was a period between the ages of fifteen and twenty when I felt angry with God and a bit distant from Him. When I was fifteen, I was in the spotlight. I had good grades; I was an underclassman who knew all the upperclassmen; and I had expensive clothes, guys crushing on me, and girls hating me. Well, one of the girls was a close friend. I had once called her my best friend. She teamed up with some other girls and came to jump me. It was a private school, and probably a sixty-second fight, but it was a fight that bothered me for a really long time. We were suspended for three days, and on the day I was due back, I was also due to start my new school. What folks didn't know before the fight was that my family and I had moved to a new district, and I was about to attend a new school. I was very mad because (1) it looked like I had run from the fight, which I desperately wanted to finish, and (2) I just couldn't understand how God would allow this experience to happen to me. I had a huge decision to make, either go back and confront my best friend and finish the fight, with the consequence of being kicked out of both my old and new school, or go to my new school with the consequence of looking like a punk. Well, as difficult a decision it was, I knew it was a matter of making the right decision over the wrong decision. I had to swallow my pride and "run" from the fight. For many years this bothered me because I felt betrayed. I lost trust in having any real friends. I felt like the cause was my being center of attention, so I figured out how to hide. I felt like God hadn't come through for me at a time when I was doing everything right to honor Him, and I just couldn't understand why He had allowed for this to happen. As a result, I just had an indifferent mind-set. I still believed in God, but I was mad at Him, so I just stop talking to Him. However, not once did I ever feel He had left me, not even during my anger. I was no longer as excited about high school. I got through things at the new school, but it was no longer really my thing, I just wanted to pass my classes, not be seen, graduate, and move on with life.

Now I was eighteen and starting college. The first year I had some sense of realization that I needed to catch up. I felt behind (a feeling I didn't used to have). In my first year, I took undergraduate courses summer, fall, and spring. By the time I got to my second year, I was exhausted! To put it in perspective, I had taken so many credits my freshman year, I was due to graduate in three years instead of four. I felt burnt out and just simply took the easiest classes I could find to get by that first semester of my sophomore year. My goal was just to maintain a 3.0 grade point average (GPA), which I did. Next came my junior year and time to declare a major, which for me was finance, meaning I had to get accepted to the Business College. I thought, *Well, that's okay. I have a 3.0 GPA.* But little did I know, the Business College had a rolling GPA admissions requirement, which meant it was based on the average GPA of the incoming class. For the class I was in, the average GPA was 3.1, and I was denied. I was devastated and thought, *That's okay. I'm a year early. I can make it up over the upcoming semester and even in the summer.* I got to the next enrollment period and was denied. Now a bit concerned, I went to a counselor, who told me I was cutting it close to the deadline and that I may need to consider another major. I shared with the counselor that I had a study abroad and could improve my grades there, which I said should be enough to get in. The counselor agreed. But after I finished the study abroad and got my grades back to apply for the Business College, I was again denied. After three attempts and three denials, I decided to give up, and my dream of walking across the stage one year earlier with a degree in finance was shattered.

I called my dad to share what was going on, and he said, "Don't tell yourself no. Let the people tell you no. Set up another appointment to meet with the business adviser, and let her tell you no." I thought, *Well, they've already said no three times, but whatever. I'll at least set up the appointment to get the official no.* In the meantime, my sister was bringing home these gospel tapes from a church she was attending. They were about faith. I decided to listen to them. I sat in my mom's living room to listen to one of the tapes, putting my faith in God to find myself walking across the stage one year earlier with my degree in finance. The instructions of the pastor who was speaking on the tape were, "Even if you do not have any money to sow, don't worry; sow your desire instead." He said, "Write whatever you were believing God for on the back of an envelope and sow that." So that's what I did: I wrote down, "To walk across the stage this upcoming May with a degree in finance." It was January, and I hadn't been accepted to the Business College. There was a part two to the message on the tape, which I told God I would listen to when I made it back to school.

I got back to school, and a few friends called to say they were going out and to ask if I wanted to join them. I instantly said, "Sure, let me get ready." Once I'd agreed, the Holy Spirit reminded me of my word that I would finish listening to the message, so I called my friends back and told them I couldn't attend, saying that I had to listen to this message. That night, that's what I did, and I was set on fire for God. Well, that next day was my appointment with the business adviser, and all I could think about was the message from the night before. I couldn't prepare what I was going to say or think of how I was going to convince the adviser. No other thoughts popped up except, *When it is impossible to man, praise God; you have now entered the realm of miracles.* I went to the meeting excited and open to receiving whatever the woman had to share. She said, "Give me one second. Let me pull up your record." She clicked a few buttons then said, "You're in."

I said, "Wait ... what?! Are you sure?"

She said, "Yes, you got a 4.0 in one of your summer classes, which boosted your GPA well above what you need to get in this semester."

To clarify, I asked, "Does that mean I can walk across the stage this May with a degree in finance?"

She answered, "Yes, that is what that means."

I was twenty-one years old, walking out of that office with only one thought: *God. When it is impossible to man, praise God; you have now entered the realm of miracles.* It was the moment I realized that God had never left me, and He had allowed me to see that no matter how I felt toward Him, He would always be there for me. He revealed to me that what I'd perceived as His not coming through for me was purposed to reveal my pride and to teach me how not to be so prideful. It was truly His grace that allowed me to receive a miracle that I believed Him for. It was my trust and obedience that allowed me to have faith in His Word and ultimately to reap what I had sown.

Leading with the Opposing Deed

As a quick recap, to have faith is to have complete confidence, to trust. Most people, when they think about the opposite of that, arrive at fear. Fear, according to the *Merriam-Webster Dictionary*, is "an unpleasant often strong emotion caused by anticipation or awareness of danger or anxious concern." Fear can also be interchanged with worry as it is the response you have when you are afraid. As we learned in an earlier chapter, worry is an indicator that you're not worshipping. Your attention is focused on the thing or on your doing the thing, and not on God and what God is doing. If you are fearful, you're not being faithful as you are lacking trust in God's Word. Now it's essential to understand that fear is a natural response, so an understanding of how fear is triggered in you is crucial. It's not to beat yourself up and question why you can't just be strong. It's trying to understand what's causing the worry and learning God's Word, trusting His promises as they relate to that fear. Remember, fear is a response of the flesh, so you must hold yourself accountable for your actions by identifying where you are leaning on your own understanding and not God's. It is essential to know that the deed of the flesh as it relates to faith is self-reliance (or selfish ambition). It's you trusting either God or someone or something else. When you are relying on yourself to do something you've never done before, it's scary. You have no previous experience to stand on and no word or promise telling you it's okay and that what you're going through is part of the process. Fear kicks in when you reach the end of your knowledge and you have no further experience to extend your ability so as to believe it's possible and to trust the process. At this point, you have one of two choices: either doing it afraid to see what the outcome will be, or having faith in God's Word, knowing that His grace is sufficient for you to succeed.

We read in Galatians 3:2 (ESV), "Let me ask you only this: Did you receive the Spirit by works of the law or by hearing with faith?" As you reflect on that question, it is important to remember that faith comes by hearing and hearing the Word of God. To receive the Holy Spirit, we must repent and surrender to God daily (as we must be filled with the Holy Spirit daily). It is our faith that we have received from the Spirit that guides us, enables us, and strengthen us to do the work. When this is your perspective, it's difficult to worry or be afraid of the work because you know it's not you doing it anyhow. It's by God's grace and the guidance of the Holy Spirit that you are enabled to do the work. The moment your focus shifts to your thinking that you must figure it out and do the work yourself is the moment you are no longer trusting God's Spirit to guide you. You are now relying on yourself to do the guiding.

When I started the executive leadership development program, I knew that it was my faith and trust in God that had gotten me the job. I could hold on to the promise that what God starts, He will finish. I started with a level of confidence that told me anything was possible because God was on my side. Well, as the year went by and I realized I was in over my head, which in hindsight I recognize was the moment I took my eyes off God, pure panic and fear set in. I wasn't sleeping, eating, exercising, or talking to family. All I was doing was working and crying, thinking, *How will I get this project done?*, realizing I had never done what I was being asked to do. I had short deadlines and no one to call to show me how to do the things I needed to do. To say that I was feeling overwhelmed and anxious is an understatement. One day I cried to God, praying for Him to show me a way. Desperate for an out, I was looking for an opportunity to get all my to-dos done. I prayed so hard and so long that I started to speak in tongues, the first time that had ever happened for me. It truly felt like an out-of-body experience. I felt my spirit being filled up and my flesh being calmed. I felt a praise come over me and a joy I can't explain that filled my heart, and all the things I was stressed out about doing became simply work that I felt confident God would show me how to do. The song that came to mind at the time, one that I listened to repeatedly when I felt tempted to take control, was "Spiritual" by Donald Lawrence & Co. Here's the hook: "You're not a natural being having a spiritual experience, but you're a spiritual being having a natural experience. … Let me be spiritual."

The moment fear or worry sets in, remind yourself to be spiritual, and go to God's Word to lean on His understanding and not your own.

Chapter Summary

To be faithful is to be fully confident and committed to what you have faith in. To have faith, you must trust, and to trust, you must believe in the result (or promise). The work we do reflects what we have faith in; it's the outcome of what we intentionally or unintentionally believed would happen. The results we get shouldn't be a surprise because the result is directly correlated to what we felt confident of and committed to doing. To lead with faithfulness requires us to be conscious of what we are and are not confident about. We must challenge ourselves when we lack the confidence to internalize God's Word regarding the matter and to identify it as the proof that is needed to trust the process and to commit to the outcome. As leaders, building trust is our number one priority. In the book *Speed of Trust* by Stephen M. R. Covey with Rebecca Merrill, the authors break down into five waves the different ways in which we establish trust, which are as follows:

1. **Self-trust.** This involves an assessment of our character and competence to discern how credible others perceive us to be, which is developed through four core elements—integrity, intent, capabilities, and results.

2. **Relationship trust.** This involves an assessment of our behavior, how consistent we are, which is what others unintentionally track. It is also an assessment of how we communicate. Are we clear or often misunderstood? Do we demonstrate respect, create transparency (unafraid to admit when we're wrong), show loyalty, deliver results, continuously improve, take on tough issues, clarify expectations, hold self and others accountable, listen first, keep commitments, and extend trust?
3. **Organizational trust.** This involves an assessment of how we utilize the trust we've built to get things done efficiently, and how aligned we are in creating structures, systems, and symbols of trust.
4. **Market trust.** This involves an assessment of our brand and whether our reputation makes others feel they can trust us.
5. **Societal trust.** This involves an assessment of our contribution, how we create value for others.

By understanding these waves, you give yourself a practical way to establish and inspire trust. It is important to note that it all starts with *self*-trust. This is important because self-trust is based on the character and competencies you have, which must be developed. God is the character developer, and His Word is a competency builder. As mentioned earlier in the chapter, we have different gifts according to the grace God has given. Trust is the faith in our ability to do the things we've been given the grace to do, thereby making faith the requirement both to receive grace and to perform our good works. The Holy Spirit's guidance allows us to build credibility, consistency, alignment, reputation, and value. It's all within our focus in gaining a fundamental truth that enables us to behave in a way that not only establishes trust but also inspires it in others. It is our faithfulness that allows us to show up as trustworthy leaders. We know that it is a direct representation of the grace God has given us, the faith that has been distributed, and the trust we've established through confidence and commitment.

Steps Forward

Think about how to apply what you've learned. Outlined below are tactical steps for you to take to allow the Holy Spirit to work and produce faithfulness in your life:

- **Identify** what you are fully confident and committed to.
- **Identify** what happened that allowed you to become confident and committed.
- **Think** about an outcome you initially felt was impossible that eventually you achieved. What made it possible?
- **Assess** what you currently believe in, and determine if you want to internalize it and have it show up in your life.
- **Identify** a scripture (choose one from the chapter or one that comes to mind through your study) that reminds you of the promises of God.
- **Repeat** the scripture until it resonates and you have memorized it.
- **Quote** the scripture daily and say it aloud so that you may hear with your own voice God's Word and internalize it (remember, faith comes by hearing and hearing the Word of God).
- **Write** down your affirmations (the things you are declaring/believing for), and find out what God's Word says about these. Ask the Holy Spirit to guide you in finding the scripture you need that aligns to God's will so you may build and apply your faith.
- **Pray** daily for God to reveal your sin so that you may repent, submit, and walk in obedience to God.
- **Thank God** for His grace and Word so that you may produce faithfulness through the power of the Holy Spirit.

End-of-Chapter Activity

Use this time to self-reflect and understand how this information is relevant to your life. Spend time with God now to worship Him and invite Him in while you answer the following questions:

1. How are you choosing to lead with faithfulness in the work you're currently doing?

2. If you currently struggle with having faithfulness, what thoughts have you formed that are keeping you from trusting? Of the things you can control, what needs to happen for you to gain trust?
3. What can you do specifically to get in the presence of God, read His Word, and learn from His teachings?
4. What one tactical step are you willing to commit to taking in order to shift the expected outcome to one you desire?
5. What makes committing to taking this one step essential for you?

Closing Scripture

"Pursue righteousness, godliness, faith, love, steadfastness, gentleness. Fight the good fight of the faith" (1 Timothy 6:11–12 ESV).

CHAPTER 8

THE FRUIT OF GENTLENESS

Rejoice in the Lord always. I will say it again: Rejoice!
Let your gentleness be evident to all. The Lord is near.
—Philippians 4:4–5 (NIV)

Chapter Introduction

When we think of gentleness, we usually think of things that are meek, soft, tender, kind. We describe gentleness as a weakness. Being gentle as a leader, especially in our Western culture, is not typically the style you want to be known for. Most would say a person's being direct, forceful, and challenging makes for a good leader because it depicts strength. This is a surface definition and also a misconception, because to be gentle is an indicator that you have a tendency not to be gentle. Think of it in the sense of being nice versus being mean. If someone tells you or reminds you to be nice, it's an indicator that you aren't nice already, that you are being mean. To use that same logic, if you are weak, and if being gentle means being weak, then why would someone tell you or remind you to be gentle? There would be no need because you are described as a weak person, meaning you're already weak. That said, gentleness is an indicator of strength. It is a person's putting forth an effort not to allow their power to get out of control and hurt someone. Biblically this is defined as "strength under control."

So why is it that when we hear *gentle*, we automatically perceive it to mean meek, soft, or tender? It is because these traits are what you display when you are gentle, so when others reflect on your gentleness, they describe it in this way. The noun for being gentle represents what it is, and the verb expresses the action of it. Noble is what being gentle is (the noun). It means you possess outstanding qualities. Appease, assuage, and disarm (the verb) is what being gentle does. It's the action you must take even to be considered gentle. It is essential to understand these differences because the doing is what the fruit of the Spirit represents. To ensure we understand gentleness, it is most critical we break down the doing of the word. According to the *Merriam-Webster Dictionary*,

- *Appease* means to make concessions to someone, such as an aggressor or critic, often at the sacrifice of principles.
- *Assuage* means to lessen the intensity of something that pains or distresses.
- *Disarm* means to deprive of means, reason, or disposition to be hostile.

Think of these three words as the actions (spiritual elements) of gentleness, which requires the Holy Spirit to humble you and suppress your strength so that you may display a level of control and tenderness to those who are being aggressive or critical and thereby bring ease to intense or hostile situations.

How do you know when you're bearing this fruit or not? Your approach is described as calm or humble, you're seen by others as a good person, always trying to do the right thing, and you focus on diffusing situations. On the other hand, when you have heated arguments or intentionally say things that hurt people and bring forth stress, you are not operating in gentleness. When you're not, it's time to ask the Holy Spirit to humble your spirit and allow you to say what needs to be said or to do what needs to be done to diffuse, or at least not escalate, the hostility.

Now you may be wondering, *Well, if I can't argue, and if I'm always known as the person who de-escalates a situation, won't others view me as weak, a pushover, someone without a backbone? Can I not stand up for myself?*

All very valid questions. And the truth is, it's about discretion, knowing when to stand up and when to stand down. It's understanding that the intent is not to get overly involved in arguing your point of view or else never getting your perspective across because you're so accommodating. Instead, it's about understanding when standing up or standing back is best for the current situation you're in. As a leader, it is important to flex your style to be gentle and direct, to get your point across without intimidation. There is a thin line between controlling your strength and not having any strength at all (i.e., being weak). Either way, to minimize the worry, you must trust God. Remember 2 Corinthians 12:9 (NIV), where Jesus said, "My grace is sufficient for you, for my power is made perfect in weakness." There is no sense in worrying about being perceived as weak, because where you are weak, God makes you strong. There's no sense in exalting your strength in aggressive situations, because, as we read in Proverbs 15:1 (NIV), "A gentle answer turns away wrath, but a harsh word stirs up anger." Being gentle is not being weak. It's being guided by God in a way that allows you to be effective, to be humble, and to have control over your strength.

Leading with Gentleness—Jesus in Action

In Matthew 11:28–29 (NIV), Jesus says, "Come to Me, all you who are weary and burdened, and I will give you rest. Take my yoke upon you and learn from me, for I am gentle and humble in heart, and you will find rest for your souls." Jesus not only displayed a gentleness but also asked us to do the same. In Matthew 5:5 (NASB), Jesus says, "Blessed are the gentle, for they shall inherit the earth." In the NLT version, *humble* is used in place of *gentle*.

Jesus has given us two key points here:

1. It is very important to be gentle and humble. By being gentle and humble, you will be blessed and inherit the earth.
2. It's challenging to be humble and gentle when you're weary and burdened (i.e., in need of rest).

The Fruit of Gentleness

Jesus shows us in Matthew 26:36–56 what it looks like to be gentle and humble during a challenging time. This verse describes a time when He was weary, having been falsely accused. With every justification not to display a gentle or humble spirit, He still did.

He said to the three disciplines He had chosen to sit and watch with Him (Matthew 26:38 NASB), "My soul is deeply grieved, to the point of death." Jesus knew it was time for Him to fulfill the prophecy of His life, which was to be crucified for our sins. He knew what was about to happen and how it was going to happen, so He walked away from His three disciples to pray that God would let this cup pass from Him and to ask that God's will be done, not His own. Although Jesus knew what and how, He was weary and burdened. At that moment, He went to the Father. He found rest and comfort in knowing that it was God's will, not His, that was getting done. In verse 45 of this chapter He said, "Behold, the hour is at hand, and the Son of Man is being betrayed into the hands of sinners." While He was talking, Judas came up to Him to kiss Him on the cheek. Jesus's response to Him was, "Friend, do what you have come for" (Matthew 26:50 NASB). At that moment, the guards seized Jesus just as one of the disciples drew out his sword and struck the man, cutting off his ear. Jesus turned to His disciple and said, "Put your sword back into its place; for all those who take up the sword shall perish by the sword. Or do you think that I cannot appeal to My Father, and He will at once put at My disposal more than twelve legions of angels? How then will the Scriptures be fulfilled, which say that it must happen this way?" (Matthew 26:52–54 NASB).

In this scripture, you find that Jesus prepares Himself and His disciples for what is about to happen. He shares the details of the critical moment, indicating that He was clear on what was about to happen, how it was going to happen, and why it was happening. Although He talks about the what, how, and why, we find that He only focuses on the why. When He talks about the what, He asks for God to allow for it to pass Him. When He talks about the how, He says, "Woe to the man who will betray me." However, when He focuses on why, He stands firm, facing the circumstance with the Word of God, saying that this is necessary to fulfill the scripture (God's will).

Often we focus on what and how, and when we do, we get discouraged. We grow weary and burdened. It is when we have arrived at that moment that Jesus says to come to Him, for He will give us rest. Jesus will listen and open our hearts to receive the why, also revealing the will of God. For when you have to do things that are not ideal or are tough on you physically, mentally, and emotionally but are for the greater good, only the why will get you through them. To fully embrace the why, you must humble yourself. Although you're capable of doing something else or finding someone else to do it, you recognize that avoiding the difficult task is not part of the plan. Jesus had the whole army of heaven (strength) behind Him. However, He suppressed it to fulfill God's will. That is, He used His gentleness to control the situation in such a way that allowed the why to prevail. You may have the strength to stop those around you or a situation from happening. However, if what's happening is meant to save others, it's meant for you to control that strength by allowing it to happen. Remember, Jesus said in Matthew 26:53–54 (NASB), "Do you think that I cannot appeal to My Father, and He will at once put at My disposal more than twelve legions of angels? How then will the Scriptures be fulfilled, which say that it must happen this way?" Jesus didn't dwell on His friend's betrayal. He willingly went with the men, not because He was excited or too weak to stand up for Himself, but because He knew that what was happening was bigger than Him and was necessary to fulfill God's will.

Key takeaway: Jesus's gentleness allowed Him to save us instead of Himself.

Guiding Principles:

1. **Have a small group.** Jesus chose three disciples to sit and watch while He went off to pray. Although He had twelve disciples, He only wanted three to see Him in His most vulnerable state, a state of weariness and burden.
2. **Have quiet time with God.** Although Jesus had friends near whom He could have confided in, He went off to be alone with God and to confide in Him.

3. **Be specific with your prayer request.** Jesus specifically asked God to let this cup pass from Him (to give Him another way). However, He declared that if His request was not God's will, then God should refrain from granting it. Ultimately, Jesus didn't let what He wanted and what He was praying for interfere with His purpose, so He ensured that if His request wasn't God's will, it would not be provided.
4. **When you're weary, go to God.** Take your "what" and "how" to God so that He may make plain the why.
5. **Know that betrayal is part of the plan.** It's the opportunity to reveal who you are in Christ by accepting it and knowing that it was necessary.
6. **Don't let your friends get caught up in saving you from taking on unwanted circumstances.** Always ensure those around you do what's right even if they seek to do wrong in support of you.
7. **Have faith in God's plan.** Recognize that you don't need to be defended or fought for because God is allowing it to happen. And if God allows it, then it's for the good of those who love Him.
8. **Focus on the why.** You know what and how, but neither will bring you comfort. Focus on the why, because the why helps you understand the importance of the fulfillment.

When you find yourself in a situation that you didn't ask for and it stresses you out, do not get angry or try to figure out how to shut it down. Just take a step back to assess where you are in the situation, and then determine how to proceed. Do you need to separate yourself from the broader group? spend quiet time with God? accept the betrayal (being thrown under the bus)? stop your friends from getting in trouble for defending you? have faith in God's plan, not yours? focus on the why? It's guaranteed that we will all have to face a trying time, a time when we hope for another way. It is at these times that we have to know that if God is allowing it, it's meant for a purpose, for salvation. Don't let your ability to save yourself keep you from fulfilling God's assignment for you. The gentleness you develop will allow you to access your purpose.

Personal Reflection

Ecclesiastes 11:5–6 (NIV) states, "As you do not know the path of the wind, or how the body is formed in a mother's womb, so you cannot understand the work of God, the Maker of all things. Sow your seed in the morning, and at evening let your hands not be idle, for you do not know which will succeed, whether this or that, or whether both will do equally well." This scripture gave me a revelation of what gentleness means. To be honest, I struggled with understanding how to be gentle. Yes, people know me to be a nice person. I have been described as a sweet, soft-spoken person, considerate, and loving; however, none of those things make me gentle. During a time when I felt like giving up, when I was annoyed by my manager's lack of ability to lead, all I wanted was to inform those around me about what wasn't working and what wasn't getting done and to expose all the negative elements of my situation. I started to think and question why I had jumped from the frying pan into the skillet. Then I started writing this chapter on gentleness and studying the Word. While trying to do it God's way and refraining from complaining, exposing others' mistakes, and informing leaders of my frustration, I found myself becoming demotivated and annoyed. Instead of changing my heart, I was trying to force myself to change my mind, thinking, *This isn't so bad. Just be who you've always been, nice, sweet, and loving.* However, the more I tried, the more I saw those around me rolling their eyes and starting to question my performance and effectiveness. I really didn't think it was me; it was the lack of vision and structure to move forward powerfully and positively effectively. Our team was in complete disarray, everyone frustrated and annoyed, everyone tired and hoping for the next role, wanting and looking to be saved. I came home and cried after weeks of trying to be gentle. The very next morning, I woke up at 4:30 with God on my mind. I prayed for God to meet me in the moment to reveal my next steps and move me forward, when I found a message by Pastor Steven Furtick called "The Blessing of Both." His opening scripture was Ecclesiastes 11:5–6, and it hit me differently than it ever had before. As he preached, he said a couple of things that really resonated with me:

1. There's a need for the structure and the Spirit.
2. Don't judge people whose shortcomings are exposed.

It was at this moment I realized that what I was going through was what I had prayed for, and right when the hardship showed up, I was quick to discredit it, and I prayed to move on to something else. However, the blessing is in both the position I was led into (what I had prayed for—Spirit-guided) and the hardship (the dysfunction I was experiencing—lack of structure). I was busy judging the experience and the person, trying to sort out the good from the bad, when God allowed both. I prayed for the blessing, but with blessing comes opposition. I could have remained focused on the opposition, which was keeping me stuck in the negativity, causing me to do nothing that would positively move the team or me forward. I felt like there was no point in doing the work because of my frustration and justification of the experience. I became idle. This scripture reminded me to keep sowing, to keep working, as I don't know how God is using this experience to develop and change me. I realized that no longer should I try to be gentle but to show my gentleness by not judging a person for what he or she is unable to do. I was getting frustrated because the situation was making my life more difficult, when the reality was that it just was not my turn to be that person. We're all that person at some point in our lives, and to be judged for a shortcoming that is exposed is simply unfair. Instead we all should extend the same grace and mercy God has given to us. So being gentle was no longer about holding my tongue or being nice when I wanted to be mean. Instead I reached the understanding that it is about continuous sowing. Only God knows how any particular experience is supposed to work for good. Judging others for their shortcomings isn't fair because we all have shortcomings. It's about being aware of when *you* have stopped working or are no longer sowing instead of when others around you aren't working. The experience is yours, and to have gentleness is to know and accept that no matter how you choose to categorize it, good or bad, God blesses both.

Key takeaway: Gentleness isn't a behavior, it's a stance. It's taking the good with the bad and appreciating the experience that God has allowed you to experience. There's a blessing in accepting both the positive and the negative.

As we think back to Jesus in the garden, a trying time for Him, we see that Jesus, too, was faced with both the good, fulfilling the scripture and saving souls for the kingdom of God (God's will), and the bad: betrayal by a friend, and eventually being beaten and crucified to death. Jesus mentions in the scripture how He could have called upon heaven to save Him. Instead, He accepted the "bad," the circumstances of His fulfilling God's will. Although Jesus went through this situation, He came out on the other side alive and with victory. He defeated death and saved us from sin. If Jesus had decided not to accept His friend's betrayal, the beating, and the crucifixion (the bad), then we wouldn't have the opportunity to be saved (the good). His gentleness was in knowing that He couldn't separate the two, because without both the outcome wouldn't be possible.

As you think about your life and the situations you face as a leader, how often do you find yourself looking at the circumstances of a situation, deciding whether you should move forward with it? During these times, your leadership is most needed because it is during this time that understanding the why becomes essential. Focusing on the bad only distracts you from reaping the good of the situation. In these moments, go to God and ask Him to reveal to you the path forward and allow for you to endure the pain. Now reflect on the moments you have decided to tolerate pain for gain. What was the outcome? Are you ultimately glad you went through it and made it out on the other side? Every time you're faced with a trying time, or when you see someone else in that situation, lead with gentleness. Be aware (through dialogue with God) and make others aware of not only the bad but also the good because the blessing is in accepting both.

Leading with the Opposing Deed

We have defined gentleness as strength under control. The opposite of that is strength not under control, which translates to anger. The opposing deed of gentleness is anger. When we are angry, we allow our feelings to get the best of us, which forces us to forget about the good of the situation and only focus on the bad. We have a decision to make, to outpour either love (a display of gentleness) or fear (a display of anger). As a leader it is important to keep in mind how you show up, because as you know, perception is reality, and the reality is that those surrounding you typically see the pros and cons in a given situation, weigh out the good and bad, and look to you to see how you handle it, knowing that you understand it's a time for control, not dysfunction. The presence of control is a conquering stance. It says that we're up against what seems to be an impossible task. However, together we're going to win and come out on the other side, better and stronger. Whereas dysfunction is a stance of fear that creates conflict and critics. When you're upset, it is tough to defuse conflict and disarm critics because of the simple fact that you are unable to see past the bad. As stated earlier in the chapter, gentleness requires a person to appease, assuage, and disarm, which are all impossible tasks for an angry person.

I would like to bring back to your attention that anger is also the opposing deed of joy. In order to identify whether you're being gentle in a given situation, ask yourself if you are allowing the situation to steal your joy. If the answer is yes, then you must refocus. As mentioned in my personal reflection, I noticed personally that I was only focusing on and wanting to change the bad, but it was in accepting that the good would come with the bad that allowed me to react in a different way. It allowed me to see the blessing of both and that the two must grow together if I am to realize the victorious outcome. That said, gentleness requires you to fix what you're focusing on to endure the pain for gain. To help you with this, I ask that you go back to chapter 2's "Leading with the Opposing Deed" and ask yourself those questions. To be gentle, you have to humble yourself and know that it's not your will to be done but God's, which ultimately means trusting that He's not going to put more on you than you can bear and also that it will all work for the good. This stance allows you to be gentle and to have joy.

Becoming angry as a result of dysfunction leaves you in a place of frustration, hopelessness, and ineffectiveness. It makes those around you feel you're the problem, which distracts you and them from the solution and impairs your ability to move forward. When you start to feel defeated to the point that you no longer see how God has blessed you, it is time for you to think about your focus. Go to God and ask Him to reveal why this situation is essential. It is only in the why that you find the help to move forward in love, joy, peace, patience, kindness, goodness, faithfulness, and gentleness.

Chapter Summary

To recap, we learned that gentleness is strength under control. It is having the ability to appease, assuage, and disarm. It's not being soft, tender, and what most misconceive as weakness. It's understanding when to step down and step forward to see the blessing in both the good and the bad of your situation. Gentleness can only come from God. Jesus asks that we come to Him, saying that when we feel weary and burdened with the promise, He will give us rest. That rest is key to controlling our strength. God said in Matthew 5:5 (NASB), "Blessed are the gentle, for they shall inherit the earth." Jesus made sure we have the means to understand that being gentle isn't just a nice thing to do but a necessity. To be gentle means to be blessed with the earth. To understand how big that is, it is important to understand what the word *inherit* means. According to the *Merriam-Webster Dictionary*, *inherit* means "to come into possession of or receive especially as a right or divine portion." Jesus tells us He is gentle and humble and also tells us, "Blessed are those who are gentle, for they will possess or receive the rights to the earth." As a son or daughter of the heavenly Father, it is important for you to know what your inheritance is, whom you come from and what was passed on to you to receive. Think of a will as an example. A father passes away. In his will he had put a clause that his daughter may not receive her inheritance of one billion dollars until she gets married to the love of her life. At first the daughter feels that this is an impossible task because she's not even dating. Furthermore, she doesn't believe in love or think she will ever be one to fall in love. However, the fortune is worth her trying. At first she thinks, *I can just take a guy up to the law office and pretend we're in love. They'd never know.* but when she and her pretend fiancé talk with the lawyer, he denies them. A few months later she comes back with a guy she's been dating for a little while, having rehearsed what each of them will say. This feels different to her because she likes this guy. However, when they go and talk to the lawyer, he smiles and thanks them for coming in but denies her again. Upset and annoyed, she decides to forfeit her fortune, telling herself that this stipulation is evidence that her father didn't really love her, that he knew she would never find the love of her life to marry, so she should simply forget it.

Ten years go by. Having received no word from the daughter, the lawyer decides to find her. He learns that she's married with two kids. She's living a mediocre life but is satisfied and happy with the life she has. The lawyer asks if she remembers him. Jokingly she says, "Yes, you're the guy who refused to give me my fortune." The lawyer smiles back at her and says, "Yes, that's me, the guy who wouldn't give it because he knew you'd inherit it. Here's your fortune. Do with it as you please."

Jesus has shown us how to inherit our fortune. He not only has been an example of what to do but also is a resource to help us do what He has done. Always remember that an impossible task is only impossible because it needs supernatural intervention to achieve. God has given us His Spirit to work in us and through us to accomplish the impossible. Being gentle is impossible when you're upset, criticized, or in a hostile situation. However, with the Holy Spirit, He focuses you and allows for you to say and do the right things to ease the situation and make peace. Let God work in your life and help you to do the impossible.

Steps Forward

Think about how to apply what you've learned. Outlined below are tactical steps you may take to allow the Holy Spirit to work and produce gentleness in your life:

- **Identify** what is making you frustrated. You know what would make the situation better, but the person who needs to listen isn't open to hearing what you're trying to tell him or her.
- **Identify** what happened that allowed you to become frustrated and angry.
- **Think** about the pressure the other person may be under and how you would act if you didn't know the solution to relieve the conflict.
- **Assess** what you can do to show the person you understand what he or she is going through.

- **Identify** a scripture (choose one from the chapter or one that comes to mind through your study) that reminds you of Jesus's gentleness.
- **Repeat** the scripture until it resonates and you have memorized it.
- **Quote** the scripture daily and say it aloud so that you may hear with your own voice God's Word and internalize it.
- **Write** down your affirmations (the things you are declaring/believing for), and find out what God's Word says about them. Ask the Holy Spirit to guide you in finding the scripture you need that aligns to God's will that you be gentle in a situation you don't know how to be gentle in.
- **Pray** daily for God to reveal the why, your action, and your next steps to release any weariness or burdens you have and to show you how to be gentle and humble in this given situation.
- **Have faith** in God's plan and Word so that you may produce gentleness through the power of the Holy Spirit.

End-of-Chapter Activity

Use this time to self-reflect and understand how this information is relevant to your life. Spend time with God now to worship Him and invite Him in while you answer the following questions:

1. How are you choosing to lead with gentleness in the work you're currently doing?
2. If you currently struggle with being gentle, what is it about the situation you keep replaying over and over in your mind that prevents you from being gentle? What about those thoughts makes you angry? Of the things you can control, what needs to happen for you to move forward peacefully?
3. What can you do specifically to get in the presence of God, read His Word, and learn from His teachings?
4. What one tactical step are you willing to commit to taking so as to shift your frustration to understanding?
5. What makes committing to taking this one step essential for you?

Closing Scripture

"You should be known for the beauty that comes from within, the unfading beauty of a gentle and quiet spirit, which is so precious to God" (1 Peter 3:4 NLT).

CHAPTER 9

THE FRUIT OF SELF-CONTROL

> *So I say, walk by the Spirit, and you will not gratify the desires of the flesh. For the flesh desires what is contrary to the Spirit, and the Spirit what is contrary to the flesh. They are in conflict with each other, so that you are not to do whatever you want.*
> —Galatians 5:16–17 (NIV)

Chapter Introduction

When we hear "self-control," we're already convinced that the onus is on us. We put so much pressure on ourselves to have discipline, to "just do it." When we fall short in either our discipline or just doing it, we tell ourselves we should have tried harder. We regularly beat ourselves up for not having self-control, not fully understanding where it comes from. We get distracted by the name "self," which obviously means "me," "myself," "I." But according to the *Merriam-Webster Dictionary*, *self* is defined as "an individual's typical character or behavior, an individual's temporary behavior or character; a person in prime condition." The definition indicates that *self* is a typical or temporary behavior, that it is a condition, not a person.

Well, if self isn't a person (me), this would mean that self-control doesn't mean "me-control," which gives us further proof that the act of self-control isn't the act of me controlling me.

So how should we conceptualize the meaning of self-control?

The *Merriam-Webster Dictionary* defines *self-control* as "restraint exercised over one's own impulses, emotions, or desires." Some synonyms for self-control are *constraint*, *self-discipline*, and *willpower*. Putting the two definitions together, we learn that "self" is a behavior or condition, and control is the power to influence or direct behavior, thereby making self-control an influenced or directed behavior or condition. As mentioned, self-control is the act of exercising restraint over or, said differently, not giving in to our impulses, emotions, or desires. It is crucial for us to understand that having self-control does require resistance. It takes resisting the urge to do what we're driven to do (our impulses), what we feel like doing (our emotions), or what we want to do (our desires). In order to resist something, we have to accept or submit to something else.

For example, when my manager asks me to do a project that I don't see the benefit of doing, every time she asks for an update, I have a strong urge to tell her she's wrong and incompetent at her job. However, I have one of two choices. One, I can tell her exactly that and accept the consequences, or two, I can resist the urge to say that and submit to the fact that she is my manager who asked me to perform a task. Instead of acting on my urge, I choose to provide the update and engage in the conversation, even though I don't want to.

Submission is what allows me not to act on the impulse to tell my manager she's wrong and incompetent, and to ignore my desire of not wanting to do what she has asked. To understand this better, we must understand what submission means. According to the *Merriam-Webster Dictionary*, submission is the condition of being submissive, humble, or compliant. To be submissive, we have to submit to others; to be humble, we have to eliminate pride; and to be compliant, we have to obey. Self-control is a condition of submission in which we are required to behave in a way that is submissive, humble, and obedient. We learned at the very beginning of *The Spirit-Led Leader* that the fruit of the Spirit comes from God. Since self-control is a fruit of the Spirit, we know that self-control, a condition of submission, comes from God. In 2 Timothy 1:7 (NIV), we read, "For the

Spirit God gave us does not make us timid, but gives us power, love, and self-discipline." Self-discipline (the synonym for self-control) is the ability to correct or regulate ourselves for improvement. Understanding this, we know that self-control is spiritual. It is something God gives us, which brings us to the question, what happens when we fail to have self-control? Why does it feel like a choice, a decision that has to be made?

Earlier we described self-control as an influenced behavior with the underlying requirement that we must decide what we will allow to influence our behavior. On the surface, you may instantly go to defining the things that influence you. But to make it simple and ensure we're on the same page, I put forth that the things that influence you are either your flesh or your spirit. Flesh is your impulses, emotions, and desires, whereas your spirit is guided by the Holy Spirit. As it is stated in Galatians 5:16–17 (NIV), "So I say, walk by the Spirit, and you will not gratify the desires of the flesh. For the flesh desires what is contrary to the Spirit, and the Spirit what is contrary to the flesh. They are in conflict with each other so that you are not to do whatever you want." Recall that the meaning of self-control involves the condition of submission. When we walk by the flesh, we gratify or carry out the desires of the flesh (what we want) instead of the desires of the Spirit (what God wants for us). According to this scripture, what the flesh and Spirit want are in conflict with each other, so we cannot do whatever we want. This reveals the choice we have to make each morning we wake up: Do we choose what we want, or do we choose what God wants for us, which then controls what we do or get? Flesh or Spirit is the influence. By having self-control, we are choosing Spirit to influence our behavior in a way that allows us to submit to others, be humble, and be obedient.

We read the following in 1 Corinthians 9:24–27 (NIV):

> Do you not know that in a race all the runners run, but only one gets the prize? Run in such a way as to get the prize. Everyone who competes in the games goes into strict training. They do it to get a crown that will not last, but we do it to get a crown that will last forever. Therefore,

I do not run like someone running aimlessly; I do not fight like a boxer beating the air. No, I strike a blow to my body and make it my slave so that after I have preached to others, I myself will not be disqualified for the prize.

Our self-discipline is our ability to strike our flesh, not to give in or become a slave to our desires, which would lead to death. Instead, we must make our flesh the slave to the Spirit, doing God's will, choosing life. In Romans 6:23 (NIV), we read, "For the wages of sin is death, but the gift of God is eternal life in Christ Jesus our Lord." By striking our flesh (resisting our impulses, emotions, or desires), we don't disqualify ourselves from the prize of eternal life because we're choosing Spirit (God's way).

Leading with Self-Control—Jesus in Action

Philippians 2:5–8 (NIV) states, "In your relationships with one another, have the same mindset as Christ Jesus: Who, being in very nature God, did not consider equality with God something to be used to His own advantage; rather, He made himself nothing by taking the very nature of a servant, being made in human likeness. And being found in appearance as a man, He humbled himself by becoming obedient to death—even death on a cross!"

Jesus was God in the flesh. However, He humbled Himself to fully encompass what it's like to be human and serve as an example of what we're capable of being or becoming. The scripture says Jesus had a mind-set that He was not above others. Although He could have behaved in such a way to place Himself above others, He served others, which required Him to humble who He was and be obedient to God. As a result of taking on human nature, Jesus felt what we feel. However, He didn't act on His feelings. He acted on the guidance of the Holy Spirit. The critical thing to remember is that feelings arise from our environment or circumstances. However, our response to those feelings requires action, an influenced behavior.

Jesus didn't act on feelings; He acted on Spirit.

When we think about where self-control is required, we see that it starts with our feelings (i.e., our impulses, emotions, and desires). To fully understand self-control, we will look at how Jesus behaved in a submissive, humble, and obedient way:

1. Jesus being submissive

There were times in the Bible where Jesus submitted Himself not only to God but also to others way less qualified than He was and for a purpose. Luke 2:45–52 (NIV) states that twelve-year-old Jesus stayed behind at the temple while His mother and Joseph searched for Him. Once Mary found Him, she expressed her and Joseph's worries. Jesus responded with, ""Why were you searching for me? Didn't you know I had to be in my Father's house?" But Mary and Joseph did not understand what He was saying to them. Then He went down to Nazareth with them and was obedient to them. But His mother treasured all these things in her heart. And Jesus grew in wisdom and stature, and in favor with God and man." Although Jesus was fully God and fully man, He recognized that He was assigned to the authority of Mary and Joseph. Although He was about God's work (not doing anything wrong), He had worried them. So instead of pushing back on them and explaining His actions, He simply submitted to their authority and obeyed their command. Jesus was in the temple working, sharing His knowledge. He was ready at that moment to preach. However, He wasn't mature. He was still only a child under the authority of His earthly parents and God. He had to decide whether He would continue to do what He could, which was preach the gospel, or acknowledge that following His parents was necessary for His development and purpose.

When you submit, you're doing something someone else wants over what you want, and every time that happens, it becomes an opportune time for the devil to tempt you. Immediately after submitting, you start to get thoughts about how you could or should defend your perspective. However, in James 4:7 (NIV), we are admonished, "Submit yourselves, then, to God. Resist the devil, and he will flee from you." We often think that we are only to submit to God's authority, plan, and power, but this scripture indicates that there will be times when we have to submit ourselves to others and *then* submit to God. As mentioned earlier, submitting is to yield yourself to the authority or will of another. Submitting requires you to either surrender or abide by the opinion or authority of another. The scripture then goes on to say, "Resist the devil," which means to overcome his temptation by being submissive, humble, and obedient to the will of God.

2. Jesus being humble

James 4:6 (NIV) states, "God opposes the proud but shows favor to the humble."

In John 13:3–17 (NIV), Jesus washes His disciples' feet. He wanted to set an example and show that titles aren't important; serving is. In John 13:12–17 (NIV), we read the following:

> When He had finished washing their feet, He put on his clothes and returned to His place. "Do you understand what I have done for you?" He asked them. "You call me 'Teacher' and 'Lord,' and rightly so, for that is what I am. Now that I, your Lord and Teacher, have washed your feet, you also should wash one another's feet. I have set you an example that you should do as I have done for you. Very truly, I tell you, no servant is greater than His master, nor is a messenger greater than the one who sent Him. Now that you know these things, you will be blessed if you do them."

Jesus, the leader, humbled who He was to serve His disciples. In Mark 10:43–45 (NIV), Jesus says, "Whoever wants to become great among you must be your servant, and whoever wants to be first must be slave of all. For even the Son of Man did not come to be served, but to serve, and to give His life as a ransom for many."

3. Jesus being obedient

Jesus mentioned many times that He came to do the will of God, not His will. In John 6:38 (NIV), Jesus says, "For I have come down from heaven not to do My will but to do the will of him who sent Me." There are plenty of examples where Jesus responds in this way, which is not only Him being submissive by submitting to the will of God but also His doing God's will by being obedient. He's honoring what God has instructed Him to do. In Matthew 3:13–15 (NIV), Jesus is being baptized. The Bible states, "Then Jesus came from Galilee to the Jordan to be baptized by John. But John tried to deter him, saying, 'I need to be baptized by you, and do you come to me?' Jesus replied, 'Let it be so now; it is proper for us to do this to fulfill all righteousness.' Then John consented." This exchange was essential as it followed the order. Jesus knew He needed to get baptized to fulfill His purpose. When we think of baptism, we see it as an act of obedience, making us whole by the washing of our sins and the renewal of our life. It allows us to access God's saving grace and gives us a clear conscience regarding God. When we think about what it means to have a clear conscience, it is knowing or believing that one has done nothing bad or wrong. Baptism allows us to see God in that light. We read in 1 Peter 3:20–22 (NIV), "To those who were disobedient long ago when God waited patiently in the days of Noah while the ark was being built. In it, only a few people, eight in all, were saved through water. This water symbolizes baptism that now saves you also—not the removal of dirt from the body but the pledge of a clear conscience toward God. It saves you by the resurrection of Jesus Christ, who has gone into heaven and is at God's right hand—with angels, authorities, and powers in submission to him." When we think about the life of Jesus and of Him as our example, we realize that His baptism was a pledge to have a clear conscience toward God, not to be disobedient, and to be saved through water.

Now looking at these three examples of Jesus behaving in a submissive, humble, and obedient way, let's discuss His actions and those in-the-moment feelings and reactions to Jesus's behavior.

In the case of Mary and Joseph not being able to find Jesus, Jesus was doing God's work. He was doing what God had called Him to do, aligning His actions with God's will. However, those actions weren't in alignment with God's timing. We know this because Jesus's act created worry in His parents. They weren't aware of His actions, which made their will different from Jesus's will, which was to do the will of God. Once Mary found Him, the Bible says she questioned Him, but she treasured this moment in her heart, the Bible also says that Jesus found favor with both God and man. Jesus's submission was in His doing what was right, which yielded Him favor.

In the case of Jesus washing His disciples' feet, Jesus didn't ask for permission; He just prepared Himself and started to do. His disciples did not feel worthy, feeling as though they should be washing His feet. They were pleasantly surprised. Then Jesus taught them that it's not about being served; it's about serving others. In Matthew 23:12 (NIV), we read, "For those who exalt themselves will be humbled, and those who humble themselves will be exalted."

Last, when Jesus was being baptized, He went down to the river and didn't think that because He was the Son of God, He was exempted. He sought John out to perform His baptism. John didn't feel he was qualified to do what Jesus was asking him to do, but then Jesus convinced him that it was necessary. John's reaction was to honor Jesus's request. In this case, Jesus's obedience required someone else's obedience; it required both Jesus and John to obey the request.

Guiding Principles:

1. **Submission yields you favor with both God and man.** Submission is pleasing to those we submit to. It lets them know we hear them and obey them. We are choosing to honor their authority and allowing them to lead. Submission also enables us to honor God's way and obey His will. The requirement in both cases is to resist our flesh, which is pleasing to God because we are choosing His way and not ours. It is important to know that it is impossible to please God without faith. Making the decision to choose His way means to have faith in Him, trusting Him to lead and guide us in the right direction. Romans 8:5–8 (NIV) says, "Those who live according to the flesh have their minds set on what the flesh desires; but those who live in accordance with the

Spirit have their minds set on what the Spirit desires. The mind governed by the flesh is death, but the mind governed by the Spirit is life and peace. The mind governed by the flesh is hostile to God; it does not submit to God's law, nor can it do so. Those who are in the realm of the flesh cannot please God." By choosing our flesh, we're saying that our way is better, that we trust our impulses, emotions, and desires more than God's, and we're choosing to place our faith elsewhere and not in God. However, in Colossians 3:22, the Bible warns us not to simply obey or submit to obtain favor, but to obey with a sincere heart and reverence for the Lord.

2. **Your title doesn't matter, but your service does.** As the leader, your job is to lead by example. To have the title doesn't make you more important, it makes you more of a servant. Before you can lead, you must know how to follow, and to properly train those who follow you, you must demonstrate the behavior you want them to follow. As stated in Mark 10:45 (ESV), "For even the Son of Man came not to be served but to serve, and to give his life as a ransom for many."

3. **Your obedience is tied to someone else's obedience.** Just as important as our obedience is, others' obedience is as well. Our obedience is all tied to one another. We read in Romans 5:19 (NIV), "For just as through the disobedience of the one man the many were made sinners, so also through the obedience of the one man the many will be made righteous." Understand that our actions affect those around us and that our and others' decisions influence what happens. So not only should we be obedient, but also, we should promote obedience.

Key takeaway: Self-control comes from God, and it is a condition of submission. Although it may not always feel like something we want to do, it is something that God wants us to do. You will know you are operating in this fruit when you have favor, serve others, and promote obedience by being obedient.

Personal Reflection

I started a new position at a new company, and at first the job truly felt like a breath of fresh air. I had more authority to make decisions and I was closer to the top, so there weren't a lot of hoops to jump through to get things done. I was getting a lot of recognition for the work I was doing. If I had to describe it, I would say it felt like Peter walking on water. I was focused on God, waking up faithfully to pray and have morning devotion. As a result of that time with Him each morning, I was able to stride and perform work miracles every day.

Eight months in, I got an offer to expand my role and move to a city my husband and I were already planning to move to. It felt like things were really falling into their rightful places. Then little by little, I got extremely busy with the move while balancing the job. This created the illusion that I was too tired to wake up before work to do morning devotion. I started to wake up to spend time with God inconsistently. Then my grandmother passed, someone who had been keeping watch over me since I was six weeks old. One month later, my other grandmother passed, and in the midst of all that, I found out that I was expecting my first child. Needless to say, I was a bit distracted. I noticed that my morning devotions and times with God were getting slimmer. I knew that all the things that were happening were not good enough reasons to turn away from God but were the very reasons to turn toward Him. The mornings I pushed myself through the fatigue of pregnancy or the grief I felt, God blessed me with energy and a positive perspective.

During this time, I noticed my manager and peers would constantly ask what I was working on. I felt like there was a whisper that I wasn't performing, that my approach wasn't effective. I was always frustrated with the chaos and confusion happening with the new position. It was clear that the new role wasn't fully thought out or crafted for anyone to take it on. I was getting pulled into gossip, which I never used to hear, and struggled not to partake in it. It was a time when I felt that my breath of fresh air had been snatched from me. I realized that within all this, I had lost my focus. A lot had changed. In reality, what really had changed was that I was focusing on everything happening around me. I was focused on all my circumstances instead of on God. I felt like Peter walking on water when he started to sink because he took his eyes off Jesus. I quickly started to realize that all the outcomes I was experiencing were directly related to where I was focused. So I started going through the process of refocusing. I woke up each morning to pray and spend time with God. I went to work focused only on being a light to those around me, leaving my fatigue, grief, and ill feelings about the job at home. I started to feel better, to have peace, and to hear less talk about my performance and the chaos in the office.

Then it was time for my performance review. My (new) manager, whom I had been supporting for about four months now, had to connect with my old manager to give me a full-year performance review. The review was the worst I'd had in all my time working. I was told that I was not inclusive and not a good communicator, that I struggled to collaborate, was aggressive, and was unable to take feedback. As I was taking notes on what my manager was saying, all I could think was, *Whom is she describing?* I have always been told I have amazing soft skills and that I'm very inclusive, a team player, and very collaborative, able to implement feedback quickly. The very essence of who I am is calm and collaborative. DiSC, a behavioral assessment, rated me as an S, which means steadiness. This is a person who is described as being even-tempered (not aggressive), accommodating, patient, humble, and tactful, someone who prioritizes collaboration, supporting others, and maintaining stability. To say I was shocked by my manager's assessment of my performance was an understatement. However, I listened and took notes. I tried to relate to the feedback and find the truth in it, but honestly I just couldn't. I found it extremely difficult to stay silent. I wanted to defend my position and let my superiors know that they had completely gotten it wrong. I tried telling myself, *Just go to work and be who you are. Don't allow this feedback to change you just because you're upset.* I struggled to go to work with a smile on my face and be a team player. The Holy Spirit then revealed Matthew 26, "the plot against Jesus," specifically verses 59–63 (NIV), which state, "The chief priests and the whole Sanhedrin were looking for false evidence against Jesus so that they could put him to death. But they did not find any, though many false witnesses came forward. Finally, two came forward and declared, 'This fellow said, "I am able to destroy the temple of God and rebuild it in three days."' Then the high priest stood up and said to Jesus, 'Are you not going to answer? What is this testimony that these men are bringing against you?' But Jesus remained silent." It was one of the few times Jesus did not speak. Although false witnesses came up against Him, He did not defend Himself, because He knew that the false pretenses were necessary if He was to fulfill His purpose. As I related my situation to this account, I realized that what was being said about me was necessary to fulfill my leadership purpose and that I should just remain silent. If Jesus could be wrongfully accused and remain silent with a response that allowed what was going to happen, to happen, then who was I to feel the need to defend a false claim against me? My self-control was tested, and it took being in God's presence to overcome the test. I realized that restraining myself from being who I'm not in order to prove who I am was the Holy Spirit working on my self-control in my work life.

The potential outcomes were simple. If I reacted or defended myself, I would prove that I was aggressive and unable to take feedback (my superiors' claim). However, if I didn't react, I would prove my character to be true, which was the most effective use of my time. I realized the true struggle wasn't defending myself. It was the pure thought of my managers thinking I had improved, that their leadership had allowed me to make this 180-degree turn. This is where the Holy Spirit reminded me to humble myself. He told me not to worry about who thinks they should get the credit but to focus on the fact that Jesus died and was buried in order to rise again and defeat death. In the end, it doesn't matter who thinks they should get the credit, because it will be abundantly clear that the glory belongs to God. Because of this, there won't be room to give anyone else credit for the good works you perform.

Leading with the Opposing Deed

Romans 8:7 (NKJV), "Because the carnal mind *is* enmity against God; for it is not subject to the law of God, nor indeed can be." In the Christian Standard Bible (CSB), the verse is phrased this way: "The mind-set of the flesh is hostile to God because it does not submit to God's law. Indeed, it is unable to do so." And lastly the Contemporary English Version (CEV) presents the verse thusly: "Our desires fight against God, because they do not and cannot obey God's laws." I share all three interpretations so that we may better understand what Romans 8:7 means. The New King James Version says, "The carnal mind is enmity against God" with carnal mind meaning worldly mind (our thoughts that are not of God), which is enmity against God. Note that enmity is a deed of the flesh. In Galatians 5:19–21, we read, "Now the deeds of the flesh are evident, which are: immorality, impurity, sensuality, idolatry, sorcery, enmities, strife, jealousy, outbursts of anger, disputes, dissensions, factions, envying, drunkenness, carousing, and things like these, of which I forewarn you, just as I have forewarned you, that those who practice such things will not inherit the kingdom of God." Understand that a carnal mind is the thoughts that are not of God; it is the mind-set of the flesh or our desires, which are hostile toward God. We fight against Him because our desires do not submit to Him and cannot obey His laws. This is the very reason that the opposing deed to self-control is enmity. Enmity is when we actively oppose or feel hostile toward someone or something. Based on Romans 8:7, it indicates that every time we have a mind-set of the flesh, we are actively opposing God. When we think back on what self-control is, we recall it is a condition of submission. To have self-control requires us to be submissive, humble, and obedient. However, when we are focused on our desires, we are unable to submit to God's way and cannot obey His requests. We read in Romans 8:8 (NKJV), "So then, those who are in the flesh cannot please God." This lack of self-control makes us hostile toward God and hence unable to please Him. By praying and knowing the Word of God, we can renew our minds and become spiritually minded. Romans 8:6 (NKJV) says, "For to be carnally minded is death, but to be spiritually minded is life and peace." We must recognize that it is our natural thoughts (our carnal mind) we must have restraint over, because the carnal mind is where our impulses, emotions, and desires arise from. This is the very area we must have control over, which we can only have through the power of the Holy Spirit.

Chapter Summary

In this chapter, we learned that self-control is a condition of submission. That self-control is not our ability to control ourselves, but a decision between two choices, spiritual or fleshly. The choice we choose, dictates our outcomes. The spiritual choice requires us to be submissive by submitting our will and ways to those of others and God, being humble, not allowing pride to get in the way of our service, and being obedient to our leaders and God. Our fleshly choice requires us to focus on ourselves, thinking and acting on our impulses, emotions, and desires, deciding that we will do it our way with no regard to how it may make others feel and/or to the outcome of pursuing our own way. These two choices are not simultaneous. It is always one or the other, so we must be aware and conscious of what we're doing and how we're behaving in order to know whether we're operating in the Spirit or in the flesh.

As we look to Jesus as our example, we recognize that He operated in the Spirit and led from that place. He, the Son of man and fully God, was submissive. He submitted His way to others and to God the Father, which required Him to be a humble and obedient leader. We learned that to have self-control yields you favor, because being submissive yields you favor. It is pleasing to those you submit to. Hence we must be careful that our motives for submitting are pure and that we're not submitting just for favor. To have self-control also requires us to serve. Jesus showed us that titles don't mean anything and that to be first, we must be last. Last, we learned that to have self-control, we must understand that our obedience is tied to someone else's obedience. This is important because we need to know that we are all interdependent on each other and that each of us must do our part because our part is critical to the success of the whole. Oftentimes in business, we hear that you are only as good as your weakest link, and the whole is greater than the sum of its parts, which both indicate that we must work together as a team to produce a given outcome. We were not meant to do anything alone. So as you explore the things you're working on that are not yielding the outcome you want, take notice of what it is you are doing. Is it something you are working on alone? Ask yourself where you need to become submissive. Is it that you need to consult with someone or submit your way to the way of another? Do you need to humble yourself, recognize you need help, and ask for it? Or do you need someone's willingness to obey? Maybe it's in the form of a yes that will give you a platform, more visibility, or simply the discernment to accept the help offered to you.

Remember, self-control is a fruit of the Spirit, which means it comes from God and is produced by the Holy Spirit. It is impossible to have self-control without the influence of the Holy Spirit. Given all the practical ways to have self-control, understand that the wisdom to decide and notice when you're operating in your flesh requires you to be present with God. Stay in His Word so that you may build your faith to make the right decisions. As stated in Galatians 5:16–17 (NIV), "So I say, walk by the Spirit, and you will not gratify the desires of the flesh. For the flesh desires what is contrary to the Spirit, and the Spirit what is contrary to the flesh. They are in conflict with each other, so that you are not to do whatever you want." In all the decisions you have to make, it boils down to a choice between the flesh and the Spirit. Whether or not there is an option you prefer, know that if you're doing something out of your reaction, feelings, or desires, it is of the flesh. However, if doing it requires you to submit, to be humble, or to obey, you know it's Spirit. Pray for guidance, and know that being a Spirit-led leader is about being guided by the Holy Spirit, which requires you to be present with God.

Steps Forward

Think about how to apply what you've learned. Outlined below are tactical steps for you to take so as to allow the Holy Spirit to work and produce self-control in your life:

- **Identify** what decisions you have to make, write them down, and evaluate your top-of-mind choice.
- **Identify**, for each choice you have, if it is a choice based on impulse, emotions, or desires. For every choice that is, write an *F* next to it.
- **Think** about what would need to happen or change for you to make a different choice, one that requires you to submit to either someone else or God and to be humble or obedient.

The Fruit of Self-Control

- **Assess** your comfort level in reevaluating your choice. What comes up for you (describe the feeling to yourself)?
- **Identify** a scripture (choose one from the chapter or one that comes to mind through your study) that reminds you of the choices Jesus made.
- **Write** how the scripture resonates with you and relates to the decision you have to make. Ask the Holy Spirit to guide you in finding the scripture you need that aligns to God's will, that prevents you from giving in to your flesh, and that allows you to make the choice that is in alignment to His will.
- **Pray** daily for God to reveal your actions and next steps, releasing any impulses, emotions, or desires you have to react, and to show you how to be self-controlled.

End-of-Chapter Activity

Use this time to self-reflect and understand how this information is relevant to your life. Spend time with God now to worship Him and invite Him in while you answer the following questions:

1. How are you choosing to lead with self-control in the work you're currently doing?
2. If you currently struggle with being self-controlled, what about the situation is making you feel defensive or unwilling to give in and do the thing you don't want to do? What about this situation is making your choice difficult? Of the options you have, what needs to happen for you to move forward spiritually. Does it require submission, humbleness, or obedience?
3. What can you do specifically to get in the presence of God, read His Word, and learn from His teachings?
4. What one tactical step are you willing to commit to taking in order to shift from operating in your flesh to operating in the Spirit?
5. What makes committing to taking this one step essential for you?

Closing Scripture

"Obey your leaders and submit to them, for they keep watch over your souls as those who will give an account. Let them do this with joy and not with grief, for this would be unprofitable for you" (Hebrews 13:17 NASB).

CONCLUSION

Being a leader is about being in a position of influence. Whether you have a formal leadership title or you only lead in specific areas of your life, there will always be times when you must lead. *The Spirit-Led Leader* helps you define how to lead when the opportunity presents itself. You may be expected to lead more often than others. However, if you live a life of positive influence, you will always be seen as a positive and effective leader (no matter your title or position).

As workers, we hope to reap the fruit of our labor, meaning we hope to see the outcome or reward for our efforts. This is difficult to do when we're unsure of the fruit we produce. If you take nothing else away from *The Spirit-Led Leader*, I hope you have at least gained an understanding that it is essential to know what you produce. To do this, look at how you act. What are the outcomes of your actions? Are you satisfied with the outcomes you see, or do you wish they were different? The areas in which you hoped for different outcomes are the areas that you should inspect for rotten fruit. That said, understand that although *The Spirit-Led Leader* highlights spiritual principles and outlines what it means to live and walk by the fruit of the Spirit, the point is not to cause people to be spiritual but to help professionals apply principles that allow them to reap the good (not the rotten) fruit of their labor. For the professionals who believe in God, I hope *The Spirit-Led Leader* reveals to you how to no longer be a closet Christian, thereby allowing you to live in your truth and involve God in your work without the fear of offending those you work with.

As a believer, you may initially question whether a situation is worthy enough to invite God (His Holy Spirit) in to guide you. So here's how you know, the situation is an opportunity to give God glory. Note that the purpose of the Holy Spirit is to give God glory and not for trivial things. When anything that you consider to be valuable or important happens, it is an opportune time to invite the Holy Spirit in to perform the work for the glory of God. Know that your work isn't trivial. It's where you spend most of your time, what you may become known for, and what impacts others. To be filled with the Holy Spirit, you must (1) believe God's Spirit is available to you (that He dwells in you), (2) be submissive, and (3) walk by faith. You are invited to say yes to these three things. Once you are filled with and being led by the Holy Spirit, you are under the influence of the Holy Spirit, walking out the fruit of the Spirit in everything you do.

As a Spirit-led leader, you encompass four elements: (1) faith, (2) trust, (3) grace, and (4) the Holy Spirit. These elements draw people closer to you, which brings them closer to God. By allowing God to influence you and hence your leadership, you lead with love, joy, peace, patience, kindness, goodness, faithfulness, gentleness, and self-control. By producing the fruit of the Spirit, you influence others in a positive way, which allows all involved to reap the good fruit of their labor.

I pray *The Spirit-Led Leader* serves you and deepens your impact in the workplace.

NOTES

NOTES

NOTES

NOTES

NOTES

NOTES

NOTES

NOTES

NOTES

NOTES

Made in United States
Orlando, FL
26 March 2023